Beautiful

Sprinkled, Speckled, Spackled

Snails

Beautiful

Sprinkled, Speckled, Spackled

Snails

. . . my journey from there to here.

S t e p h e n   W o l f e ,   J r .

iUniverse LLC
Bloomington

Beautiful Sprinkled, Speckled, Spackled Snails
. . . my journey from there to here.

iUniverse books may be ordered through booksellers or by contacting:

iUniverse LLC
1663 Liberty Drive
Bloomington, IN 47403
www.iuniverse.com
1-800-Authors (1-800-288-4677)

ISBN: 978-1-4917-0780-7 (sc)
ISBN: 978-1-4917-0781-4 (e)

Printed in the United States of America

iUniverse rev. date: 11/27/2013

CONTENTS

for Joey, because she listened first.

. . . my story can be summed into seven words
or less: my brain broke. I suffer from an
undiagnosed mental health affliction – a broken
mind and battered heart.

In my life of thirty-one years, I have broken a
total of one time. My definition of that broken
is losing all ability to function as a normal
person would – normal as defined by society. I
do not boast in my admittance to you that on a
certain occasion, during a certain circumstance,
I slipped – I shut down. And for three years, I
lived two totally different lives – the life I
wore in public and the life I spilt in private –
and both were afraid of the other.

I was afraid that people would see me for who I
really was. That my life was a lie, that even I
believed in. That beneath this mask of smiles
and light and personality was a mistaken reality
that I was a waste. That beneath this smile was a
struggle. That beneath my light there was dark.
That beneath my big personality just hid even
grander pain.

My life was her and when she chose to disappear
from this life of mine, I panicked - a panic so
intense that it consumed my whole self - choking
words into whimpers, smiles into smudges, love
into loss, and life into lies.

Your fear might be spiders. You may fear the
ocean or sharks. You may be scared of girls or
boys and the rejection they may give. You may
fear death or dying alone. But me, during this

three year journey, I feared me - my honesty, my truth, my frailty, my vulnerability. I feared not wanting to live, but lacking the courage to die. And that fear kidnapped me for pennies and forced me into a closet with no lit-up exit signs.

This fear consumed me - every single second, of every single day, in every single thought. And if I'm being totally honest with you, even as I type this, I dwell on this fear. Because that's the disease; that's the struggle; that's the pain - the affliction of a broken mind. There's no cure - this isn't chicken pox; you don't beat it once and it's gone forever. This is something you live with - you live in. It's the face in the mirror; it's the voice you can't ignore. It's the feelings you can't escape; it's the monster under your bed. It's the breath you inhale; it's the hand you hold - and the scariest part is that after a while, after a few million miles and a sleepless night, you become numb to it. This becomes the new normal. You accept that a good day is getting out of bed and brushing your teeth because there's no more tears to cry and no more blood to bleed - you're empty. Alone. And lost.

Soon enough, that fear transposes itself onto and into others - you begin to fear the stigma inside of others towards you. The shame, the embarrassment, the looks, the whispers, the absence of best friends - even they begin to walk on the other side of the sidewalk. And, hence, you do not seek help. You continue living this hell your mind is living within, silently. Every morning, you pick a smile-of-the-day from the empty jar in the pit of your soul and you go to work, you go to church, you do all your extra-curricular activities, in hopes that no one will notice that you're defective.

I didn't seek help, either; I wrote sentences instead.

This is my story – my journal of making sense from my crazy; sneaking into the lives of strangers, even myself.

preface

. . . I write . . .
. . . I write sentences . . .
. . . in my own diary, that graduate to I sharing
with whomever and whoever will listen, will read.

. . . these sentences congregate together,
piecing together a puzzle; pulling words from
swollen tongues and sewn lips so that those who
had a story or have a story, can finally be
heard.

. . . they are my stories. My life. My
vulnerability strewn across the yard as
wildflower seeds so maybe . . . just maybe, a
life will bloom between the concrete cracks of my
own frailty.

I am untrained.
I am not a counselor.
I am not a doctor.
I cannot prescribe drugs.
I do not offer solutions.
I do not solve equations.
I cannot put the puzzle pieces back together.
And I cannot answer 'why?'.

But I do give you my heart.
My fingertips.
My mouth.

I do grant you a chance to be heard, a chance to
tell your story.

I will love you regardless of your circumstance
that was created for you or by you.

I will get on my knees and search for every missing piece of you that has been lost and I will cheer rambunctiously as you find yourself again.

I am but a simple man who was given an uncanny gift to write the words of a silent and hurting and empty people and what I lack in education, in beauty, in personality, in wealth, I will surely give you my last whimper so that you no longer have to sorrow in silence.

I am broken, defective. I have been silent. I lost hope. But I know the joy in being found.

I've swam in the tears of rejection, I've dove into the sea of doubt, I've tasted the art of failing, I've splashed in the stink of pity, I've crawled through the pit of prejudice, I've laughed at my own lies, and I've lost my favorite part of me . . .

But I'm here today, typing this decree, spilling my own blood first, hoping that someone will stand with me . . .

. . . and while standing with me, I'm standing next to you.

. . . and now neither of us . . .

. . . are alone!

fliegen

part one – journal entries

she had a dream *Sunday, March 6, 2011 at 1:12pm*

She lives in the house
in the field
where only one horse lives.
(stop)

I sit on an uncomfortable stained couch
and wonder
if she liked where she came from?
None of her memories are up on any walls
(but maybe her memory is what she's trying to
forget).
(stop)

She enters the room
from a long hollow hallway,
walking as if she was looking for her dream.
Her face wears not even a fake smile.
Sadness and guilt seems to course thru her veins.
Her eyes stare a bullet into my soul.
(stop)

She is as marble
- beautiful,
frigid.
I am like soup,
I cannot stand.
I have an animal in my throat
that wants to scream out.
My whole self goes blue
(maybe yellow),
choking on misplaced letters and vowels
but at least
I'm not voicing a lie.
I don't know why.
I cannot understand.

I'm not living her hell
and time will not heal this you-shaped hole in
her heart.
(stop)

Gone are the days of laughing without sound,
of playing in mini-deserts called sandboxes,
of wearing ice cream stains with pride,
of believing in prayer.

She wasn't always like this -
but history happened while she brushed her teeth.
(stop)

She sat down beside of me,
as close as the petals on an unopened rose.
I waited for her to speak.
She wept like a thunderstorm
as her heart fell open
and described a scene I can't repeat.
A scene of a painted portrait of hanged hope,
of a stained carpet of a convicted conscience.
(stop)

She reached for my hand;
her fingers as soft as marshmallows.
She had a dream last night -
she was standing under a bluer than blue sky,
and there her one true love was waiting by.

dear anybody *Monday, March 14, 2011 at 4:38pm*

. . . a few weeks back, I was called upon to talk to a "disrespectful boy". As I walked thru the swinging double doors, I became keenly aware of my *inadequacy* in being able to diffuse the situation. Nonetheless, I was asked to stay with the family and serve as a mediator. Within the course of listening, I began penning the following letter. While writing such, the "disrespectful boy" grabbed my pen and asked, *"what are you writing . . . how crazy I am?"* I responded with a broken voice, *"no, I'm writing your suicide note."* With tears in his eyes, he hung his head and said *"how did you know?* (pause for fumbling of words) *. . . that I was planning on killing myself tonight!"*

The following is that letter I penned. These were phrases uttered and alluded to within the course of our conversation. I, merely, arranged them into "letter form". The phrase, *"it's not that I want to die, but I don't want to live either"*, grabs my heart and never lets go. I've spoken to too many (attempted) suicide survivors, and all agreed with this agonizing phrase - it wasn't that they wanted to die, they simply didn't want to live! I wish I could ask those who attempted and were successful - I wonder if they felt the same - I wonder if anyone dared to ask - I wonder if I could have helped!

Dear Anybody,

By the time you read this, I hope to be dead.

You can't rewind history. You can't take back that deed acted out in public and you can't swallow words after they've been spilt. I'll linger in your mind and you'll devise ways of solving the riddle of me with countless "what if's", "what could've been", "why this", and "why that", yet the answers will be swept like crumbs into a coffin. Proper etiquette requires me to scribble the words "it's not your fault, this is solely my decision", but that would be a lie. This isn't "happy ever after" - we all know I didn't get here by myself.

I don't want to wake up at 6am anymore. I don't want to take out the trash. I don't want to do my homework. I don't want to scoop the litter box. And I, most definitely, don't want to see her with him anymore. I don't want to be sad or lonely. I don't want to eat, drink, sleep, stand, walk, run, or breathe anymore. And last of all, I don't want to love anymore, wonder anymore, or think anymore.

It's not that I want to die, but I don't want to live either.

Did you really love me? Did I love you? Will you miss me? Will I miss you? And does either of us want to know the truth?

Sincerely,
a Disrespectful Boy

what's wrong with me? *Friday, March 18, 2011 at 11:47am*

. . . in an attempt to answer *"what's wrong with me?"*, I gripped my pen and poured these words.

I can count on six fingers the times within this week that the above phrase has been uttered in my ears. In "expected counseling mode", the reply to such a question ranges in or about the phrase, *"there is nothing wrong with you"*, yet rarely does that convince or change the utterers mind. The utterer thinks it in their mind, believes it in their mind, convinces it in their mind, dwells on it in their mind, thus, creating the core of their mind. Any failure of any magnitude within their life registers another tidly-wink in the *"there is something wrong with me"* tablet. Furthermore, being one of the utterers myself, I stand in the soles of the countless that have uttered said phrase. Standing in one's sole doesn't reflect a *"I know exactly what you're going through"* mentality, yet it signals a common bond of whispering *"I've been there, you can lean on me while you answer your own question and I mine."*

Thus, for investigative purposes, and using the one skill I pretend to possess as a decorator with words, I wrote my answer to my uttered question:

What is this beam in mine eye
that hides and distorts the world?
It is the lie unto thy self
that binds this oyster's pearl.

I share my answer realizing that unbelieving a fiction is a grand task. Rejection begins a revolution in the mind that becomes a lie of the grandest scheme. Rejection, inevitably, writes with a permanent marker, *"there is something wrong with me"* on our frontal lobes, but as seen with my own eyes, permanent marker doesn't really last permanently. I wrote with a blue Sharpie *"there is something wrong with me"*, on my left forearm (I'm right-handed), Tuesday afternoon. As I'm typing this on Friday morning, the *"w"* in the word *"with"* is all that smudgingly remains. Not diminishing the tragedies that have led all of us utterers to believe a lie (for some have believed the lies for innumerable years, thus extra-scrubbing may be prescribed) but for sake of a brief thought, the thesis of my science object lesson rendered this: if I don't continue to reapply the permanent marker, the words fade away. In essence, if I discontinue believing my own lie or re-adjust and altar my vantage point, I just may allow my heart, my smile, my worth, my grand-ness, my most valuable part of me, that part so few have seen because I hid it, that part that I've had locked away for only me to see, that part that God gave only to me - my pearl will amaze all that behold!

End of attempt.

unwilling actor *Tuesday, March 29, 2011 at 7:46pm*

I often entertain the musings of those who fail
to grasp what I do, and in those musings I (or
the way of my pen) am questioned, critiqued, and
ridiculed. Undeterred from my passion within, I
continue to write from a heart laid bare, for
those who do not have the answer, who have lost
their words, who do not have a voice to speak of
their "hells", not for the ignorant. I write for
those who have locked themselves away, choosing
to suffer in silence. Their longing to be heard
and understood ever increasing, yet squelched by
a fear of being judged, labeled, ridiculed, and
forgotten by a classless class. As stated by a
certain high school girl, *"it is a lonely place
in the mind of an unwilling actor"*.

I have grappled and tossed with the scene painted
below by that "unwilling actor". What follows
can be defined as "sick", "twisted", "demented",
"perverted", or any other horror adjective you
so choose, yet to this young lady, it is "life",
"truth", "reality". For this "unwilling actor",
she has suffered alone, trying to forget.

I often state "that time heals a many of wounds,
yet time fails to heal a memory". This account is
a testament to those words.

She described the following through a
thunderstorm of tears. I listened and penned
these words:

. . . kidnapped for pennies,
I chose to partake than be bound.
His eyes speak of violence,
my dress falls to the ground.

9

. . . theft of my innocence, six minutes undone;
the sheets are guilty, swallowing the dead –
like merry maggots feasting
on this memory inside my head.

This "unwilling actor" was sold to the highest
bidder, every weekend, for four years. She was
nine years old.

I write this note with an honesty that few are
willing to discuss and/or even recognize. I
struggle with even allowing my mind to venture
where this "unwilling actor" has trod, yet there
is a need and a longing in these "actors" to
break the silence, to break the chains that bind
them to their past and to seek love and refuge in
their futures. Thus, I write and shall continue
til . . .

the naked tree

. . . the tree was stripped of its clothing by an unforgiving wind; like scripting pardons on my flesh, ever-bereaved by what could have been.

Deuteronomy 2:2-3 - . . . and the Lord spoke to me, saying, You have circled this mountain long enough. Now turn north.

He showed me his arms with a reluctant pride - within the creases, hid his "sins". He told me of his release, of his reasons, all flung into the past of "what could, what should, what would have been". He was held captive by an enemy who had set base camp in his head. I lost myself in his words and became keenly aware that I am a prisoner of that same enemy.

I often counsel (consult) on the fine art of "letting go", pretending that I have mastered said "art"(Deuteronomy 2:3 references it as *"circling a mountain long enough"*), yet when listening to "he", my facade was fully exposed. Tears swelled and my head hanged as he listed "failures" of forgiveness, of forgetting, of fault. He "cut" to release his anguish. I prance and dance around mountains (mind you, the same mountain, every day, every hour, every second) to release mine. I do not let go. I have a death-like grasp on my past. I have beaten a well-worn path around my mountain.

When attempting to begin the healing process with "he", "he" helped me begin to see the "real" me. "By his fruits ye shall know him", yet here of late, I am that naked tree. I'd like to think I'm ready to go northward, that I'm ready to blossom, but . . .

seven minutes *Sunday, April 10, 2011 at 3:43pm*

The value of a quarter has plummeted.

My attention to this subject matter rested undisturbed for a countless number of uncaring years, until this afternoon, when that sleeping giant of a crux was awakened; leading me to this illuminated screen.

At Walmart, it takes a quarter placed strategically in a certain slot to purchase an inevitable piece of trash. Just yesterday, at the Army's thrift store, a quarter allowed me to purchase two stuffed farm animals – buy one, get one. And lest we forget, a quarter will forever be the pinnacle of the classic anecdote – "flip it to see who goes first".

Amazed at the frailty of copper, a chance for redemption was found at the Laundromat today.

Resting, amongst rows of rumble and tumble, was a sign that read in not one, but two languages – "7 *minutes for 25 cents*".

Startled at such a proclamation, I smiled at the possibilities.

I was seated next to a lovely lady and shifting slightly to my left, I garnered her attention. Pointing to the noted sign-age, I posed the following question, *"ma'am, if God gave you the opportunity to buy seven minutes after you die, to return to earth, would you?"* She shyly smirked and offered this response – *"I guess it depends upon where I was at."* No elaboration was received, and as she arose to tend to more important matters, bloomers and loomers, I began to chuckle at her utmost correct answer.

Meeting God on the doorstep of the Pearly Gates or the slope to Hell's Hole, would be quite the deciding factor.

After fourteen more minutes were purchased, she returned to her seat to my left and I must assume, she caught a glimpse of my smirk, prompting her to quip – *"what are you thinking?"* I pounced on the opportunity to expound on those Pearly Gates and Hell's Hole, of which led her to utter: *"I may need to use two quarters, I have much to confess."* My snappy comeback *of "well, in that case, I may need to just go ahead and redeem a whole dollar"*, was met with much laughter and smiles.

The conversation concluded without much further fanfare but an impression of the simplest kind will remain. *"7 minutes for 25 cents"*. Reality awakes to the fact that Time waits for no one. Time is no respecter of persons, and once wasted, remains in ruins. Time nonchalantly marches, encompasses the globe, and dictates our days, yet at the Market Street Laundromat, Time can be purchased in seven minute bundles for a quarter. The thought is quite splendid.

blue lawn chair *Sunday, April 17, 2011 at 11:36pm*

I was uncomfortable for twenty four hours, for Edison's gift to mankind refused to heed to my command. Lights should beam brightly with a flick of the wrist, yet I flicked to no avail.

Power outages are a common side-effect of a tornado. Loss of life may occur, as well.

(break)

One blue lawn chair. One red lawn chair. Two sisters sitting in silence until "Hi, I'm Stephen" stirred the air. I welcomed myself to an Indian style seat beside of the blue lawn chair and followed my introduction with a *"I'm here to help!"* Red lawn chair sister smiled and began to tell of a scene I can't justly describe. Yesterday she had a home. Today she had a million little blended pieces of that home. She spoke of salvaging what she could, combing her street for any evidence of a life she once possessed. She paused to compose herself and uttered softly, *"but I'm still alive, my sister is still alive, and we have each other. We'll make due on love for a while"*.

Amongst the rubble, I stumbled upon a shattered Bible. The binding of the Bible discarded. The cover missing. Pages torn, yet found, staring at the sky. I knelt down to view what chapter and verse were visible. The page exposed was crusted with mud, with a tear in the upper right corner, but these words were the first I read, *"but love covers all . . ."* - Proverbs 10:12.

Steady Eddie failed my flick, and I was
up-in-arms, until I met the two sisters in the
blue and red lawn chairs.

Amongst that sea of shredded lives, amongst
the outpouring of generosity from countless
volunteers picking up those pieces, and in the
bond between two sisters, love was covering all.

A tornado can take a life, can take a home,
can take a home full of stuff and blend it to
nothingness, but love - love remains - love
covers all.

krispy kreme eyes

Early in my education, the principle of *"not being able to help those who don't want help"* was stitched into my thinking. Furthermore, in mental health, much encouragement is derived when a patient is willing to verbalize their struggles. The task of "helping" is jump-started when the one needing help states clearly, *"it hurts here"*. Their verbalization lays a foundation to which you may prescribe a healing solution.

(break)

We met in a 20 x 16 hole-in-the-wall hotel room. Stained maroon comforter, two deceiving fluffy pillows, two matching wooden chairs designed by "jack wuz here" and "stacy loves robert", and a wobbly table with an accompanying sticky ash tray. His appearance was lost in my fixation into his krispy kreme doughnut eyes - glazed, blank, void of substance. Before my entrance, he had determined his silence, for my presence was his families cry for help, not his, but his eyes scripted these words within my journal: *His bones have been shut up. His anger and his hatred, which has led to this self-induced prison, has been tested, tempered, and fueled; and that once screaming spark has become an ill-fated silent fire, which alludes to a simplest conclusion and frightful proposition: the most fearful of men is the quiet man. For we all know of what the screaming man tells of, but that of a quiet man - oh where does his mind-steps trod?*

may 1, 2011

My eye has been on the streets, the screen, the screams, the streams. I have yet to cheer the death of a man; more or the less, the murder and assasination of a man. Granted, an eye for an eye but *"returning hate for hate multiplies hate, adding deeper darkness to a night already devoid of stars. Darkness cannot drive out darkness: only light can do that. Hate cannot drive out hate, only love can do that."* (possibly stated by MLK or Penn Jillette)

I, like you, remember September 11, 2001, vividly. I remember what I was doing, where I was doing what I was doing when the news broke. Emotions of all flavors crept into my heart and mind, even hatred. Questions were hurled at the TV, at my parents, at my professors, at the sky - all coinciding with the prevailing *"why?"*

Close to a decade removed, yet tightly-knotted together, the *"why"* is still unanswered. And as I watch the nightly news, more questions have been asked and created, than answers given. Yet, as more and more details emerge, the simplest of facts remain - yes, he is a legend amongst hide-and-seekers; yes, he is a murderer; yes, he is an evil terrorist; yes, he deserves his justice; and yes, he and I are of the same blood.

On September 11, 2001, God's heart was the first of all hearts to break. And the same can be said of May 1, 2011. I am guilty of breaking that same heart! Lest we forget, before we were "one nation under God", we were universally, "one blood under God".

blurry *Monday, May 9, 2011 at 3:39pm*

"Where there is no vision, the people perish."

(Proverbs 29:18)

I possess no such vision. My vision was her. My vision was an illusion of the grandest rainbow conjured up in memories and daydreams – cartoons even – that eluded me once I reached that sacred place where rainbows kiss the ground and skittles sprinkle the earth. Thus, my eyes are left empty, lonely, and searching.

The ground is now met with a hopeful gaze pretending that I rest beneath. The dew drops only water that expectation.

I have begat an abundance of random scenes to pursue, yet once obtained or denied, I rest knowing it was merely a pre-occupation with surviving one more day for others, not myself. I tend to wish upon my death being deemed "graceful" above "selfish", thus allowing that love for others to remain my sole reason, yet I await the day my thoughtfulness will forsake me.

I have allowed few to travel into my footprints to offer comfort, support, solace, love. Those few who have dared to enter, walk beneath my resolve that hangs as a suffocating fog: You cannot unlock the gates of this self-imprisonment, nor can you improve the conditions unto which I live. Do I a favor and kindly escort yourself from my demise, for it shall not be becomingly to stain such a charming dress!

Littered in my oxygen space are the cheery words of others. If only I could reach out and grasp those words, maybe I would have something of sustenance to cling to, but words are like carbon dioxide. A grand invention, but in excess and solidarity, it strangles the life out of you. And to be frank, words are an excuse as to why I suffer, why I bleed a spotless blood. Those words built me on a foundation of beautiful lies.

This is not a plea that I pen. This is my last resort to survive, but then again, I do not even want to participate in survival. I have mastered the theory of survival of the fittest, but surviving is not living, and I want to live.

The trade of me for something inked as the "afterlife" offers a brilliant hope. Heaven, reincarnation, virgins await. The product of death tilts the scales on the face I'll have for the rest of my life.

I am broken, defeated, poor, and used.
Glasses cannot cure what ails.
You came and saw and loved as you could,
but I am the one who failed.

For here, there is no vision.

. . . with the delightful opportunity to behold another's writing, I responded with this short reply, "*the curse of talent, trickling from your hand is overwhelming, my friend . . . your words play out like a symphony from a heart spilt, and as I too have learned, a true writer spills his own blood first.*"

Spilling your own blood first.

My blood first.

I am not the man I dared to be as a young lad. I have failed my own name. I have smudged me with a host of deplorable deeds, all dripping with lies and arrogance. With even greater shame, I have believed the very lies I've vomited. That stench lingers where I trod and I have ran much, running in place, splashing in stink, slipping on my makers, my God, myself, my love, my friends.

My noteworthy accomplishments could be written on a 3x5 index card, hidden beneath a stain of selfishness. My resume, double-spaced, fills a one-sided printers page. Interviews are sarcastic set-ups for rejection. My passion pales in comparison to experience. And a degree in Him leaves you lost but grounded and sometimes found. I never intended to be well-known-versed-traveled-and-wealthy, but I sure envisioned being anywhere other than here!

I would rather feel anything than nothing, but numbness has befallen on my heart. I pretend to possess much love, just none to give. I reach into my jar of faces and find a smile a day, but like all things that come in a jar, once the seal is broken, freshness deteriorates. My smile has soured. I have littered shards of me on a many of lives and land. Now to picking up those pieces of me, I am left with a bellowing question, "how do you put the puzzle of you together, when you don't even recognize the pieces?"

Defective. Defeated. Dejected. Disappointed. Desolate. Oh, Webster penned a definition to these adjectives, but those definitions become numb and null when they become the hell that swallows you. Nonetheless, as Barry sings, "it's only words, and words are all I have . . .", my ink begins to spill from what is left of a heart:

His eyes are bleeding out of the well of his soul,
His prayers are lost in the breeze.
His words stand up on the tip of his tongue as a
wilted flower,
His grace is spilt upon his sleeves.

His heart has fallen over and drowned in the mud,
His hands tremble as the crashing of waves on the
shore.
His stare has set on the sun in the west,
His pride perches as crumbles on the floor.

His feet are shod with the stench of yesterday,
His hope dissipates as swiftly as the morning fog.
His salvation is nailed to unseen tree,
His last breath whimpers for a forgiving God.

bicycles *Saturday, May 28, 2011 at 10:03pm*

Just above the designated peg where my
"safety-first" helmet rests, a reflection of
me caught my eye. One year ago today, this boy
looked into this same mirror with a different boy
staring back at him!

I have written much of my reliance on my bicycle
- for I gently press - my bicycle saved me when
I could not save myself. Dripped to poured,
between mile one and this nine thousandth plus
mile, I began to feel as if me plus a bicycle
could conquer the world, for *"life is like riding
a bicycle; in order to keep your balance, you
must keep moving (Albert Einstein)."* That which
made me succeed with my bicycle, is precisely
the ingredients to which I shall measure future
successes in life - the thrill of the challenge
that led me to begin, the stubborn persistence of
self that held me accountable, and the patience
that was willing to be born again when the last
stroke failed.

When quizzed upon the theory of relativity,
Albert Einstein responded, *". . . oh yes, I
thought of that while riding my bicycle."* I can
attest to no such grandeur while riding mine,
yet finding myself became the quest, and between
here and there, pieces of me were re-assembled,
re-configured, re-discovered, re-birthed!

Frances Willard said, *"(he) who succeeds in
gaining the mastery of the bicycle will gain the
mastery of life."* My mastery is limited, yet I'm
nine thousand plus miles closer than before, and
for that - I smile!

. . . a sincerest of "*thank you's*" to those who have been patient while I melted away on my bicycle. I once pretended that I was fire, but the tears on the asphalt reflected the ice of who I was – cold, alone, lost, and hardened by years of replicated fears. Those days now rest in peace, with an etched epitaph reading, "*I once was lost, but now am found! (John Newton, Amazing Grace)*"

wonderings on love

. . . the how-to of my writings was birthed from
the mouth of a legend. His wisdom has the effect
of a constant rain, soaking and penetrating
the hardest of hearts. The opportunity to sit
under his shade and absorb his words became a
foundation to which I strive within each sentence
I bleed. He littered sages on my classroom floor
that echo in the vessels of my mind everyday:
"spill your own blood first" and *"write on such
things yet unheard".*

Broaching the topic of "love" was defined as "a
pointless subject", teetering on the rationale
that anybody who is anybody can write as much.
The possibility of swooning a harlot with "roses
are red" are just as equal as a boy discovering
a girl and remix-ing those roses! I am guilty of
trying my hand as a florist, yet for a season or
two, I have had a thorn in my flesh that allows
no flowers to bloom.

Nonetheless, a fancy within me was startled,
awakened if you may, and I began to play with
words dripping with dew drops of "wondering".
No crush is without wondering. No new love is
without wondering. No happy-ever-after is without
wondering. It's that wondering that steals
your sleep, causes perspiration in undesired
locations, causes a shortness of breath, causes
you to stare longingly at your phone hoping,
praying, waiting, causes you to giggle, causes
you to smile for no notion . . . . allows you to
win. The blessings of wondering swim in a pool of
controlling the outcome. Wondering doesn't know

the difference between yay and nay, and thus on
the sunny-side up, you win every time!
(May I pause and acknowledge that doubt is a
wonder, as well, yet I'm smiling while typing,
thus I shall remain optimistic in my bleed.)

What lies below is that wondering at the beginning
of any hope of any beginning love. Yes, I too
had to re-read that sentence and slow my speech
to a southern drawl to shape sense, but I leave
it un-edited because I believe it conveys the
jumble-ness that any and all of has experienced
when wondering or hoping, praying, and waiting to
discover if he/she "likes" you/me back

I declare, this is my blood - I wrote this
staring at myself in the mirror. From the
selfishness of the first two lines, to the
puzzle-pieced heart in the next two, skipping
over to the take me as I am in the following
stanzas, and the fear of rejection in the last,
this is what wondering looks like to me . . .

(break)

leave me alone,
i want nothing more than what i am.
so don't leave me alone,
i buried it once, yet it's starting to show . . .
. . . even though, we're nothing.

take me or don't.
a three hour ride
and we got nowhere close
to west and beyond.
i want to hold your hand
and sit on that bench,
so take me or don't.

take me with you
because if it's not with you
i've nowhere to go.
believe me when i'm blue,
i promise you gold.
altho you can't say it yet,
you've never smiled so much
and it looks to stay that way,
but the first kiss always says the most.

so take me or don't!
but if we end up alone,
this kingdom is stone.
so take me or don't,
she'll love me or won't!

shake-a-sketch

Propped Indian-style in the middle of the aisle, this lad was twirling an etch-a-sketch. His mother, viewing the instructions on another childhood staple, peered downward and saw her son's handiwork. Disappointed or amused or approving or pick your own adjective, she leaned over, laid hand to etch-a-sketch, and shook it up! Picture be-gone! With a crinkled nose and sly smirk, she whispered, *"start over"*. The lad began again . . . clean screen, clear canvas, new chance.

At birth, God hands us all our very own, specialized, one-of-a-kind, etch-a-sketch. Wrapped in flesh, sustained by blood, with one direction -draw your life however you wish. He allows us to control the knobs, our decisions, our deeds, our tongue, our eyes, our desires. I boast, I've sketched a few Mona Lisa's, but in abundance, I've scribbled away a many discarded deeds, yet with both, God's unwavering hand has shook my sketch, whispering, *"this picture you're drawing has become what it had in it to become. You shall not prolong. You've created enough chaos or you've mastered that art. You're forgiven or well done. Now on to the next. Start over."*

During times of God's shaking, I've thrown my share of temper tantrums and rocks at the sky. He threw the rocks back, and watched unmoved, yet, while I may not have been finished with my poor man's Mona, God patiently cleaned my canvas, cleared my way, created my thousandth second chance I least deserved, and with a crinkled nose and sly smirk, (because momma and God always know best) whispered, *"start over!"*

back to the booth

Borrowing text from 'confessional booth', *"I am not the man I dared to be as a young lad. I have failed my own name. I have smudged me with a host of deplorable deeds, all dripping with lies and arrogance. With even greater shame, I have believed the very lies I've vomited. That stench lingers where I trod and I have ran much, running in place, splashing in stink, slipping on my makers, my God, myself, my love, my friends.*

My noteworthy accomplishments could be written on a 3x5 index card, hidden beneath a stain of selfishness. My resume, double-spaced, fills a one-sided printers page. Interviews are sarcastic set-ups for rejection. My passion pales in comparison to experience. And a degree in Him leaves you lost but grounded and sometimes found. I never intended to be well-known-versed-traveled-and-wealthy, but I sure envisioned being somewhere other than here!"

(. . . thus concludes my borrowing.)

I have prayed prayers until I started believing that prayers are of the wasted nature, a fragile figment hoping there's more than just me in this fight - a depiction of not failing alone, misery lusting for company at its finest. Accompanied with the Christmas list of my failures and rejections and prayers gone awry, were answers of finality that I deemed un-approvable, like your graded English paper with too many beet-red stray marks. I have bartered with God, drawn the short straw every time, and pleaded my sanity and rationale with the obnoxious Judge He is.

'All the world is a stage', Willie Shook said, and I find myself being God's entertainment or sitcom of choice on the SHOWtime nightly loop of graduated and canceled programming. I feel irrelevant, like *"hey God, it's me again, not that you care, but you're really starting to piss me off with not agreeing to any of my prayers or granting any of my wishes."* Granted, you're not a Genie-in-a-Bottle God, but this Omniscient God persona is getting old. Fast!!!

God has allowed me to share this viewpoint for a substantial amount of personal history. My temper tantrums have unmoved Him and He hasn't been rubbing out any of my make-a-wishes, although, He has been educating this stubborn shadow of the man I dare to be. I've learned that for every wrong answer I've been granted, 'twas the right answer to a different a question. Maybe He is listening, maybe all things do work together, maybe I'll learn to ask the right question(s), maybe I'll continue trusting Him . . . maybe I'll continue minding my own business and letting Him tend to mine.

my suicide letter

my whimper of words into wails and sentences into
scars.

. . . afforded the luxury of spilling blood to
wood, I wish to declare my sanity in all that
I shall pen, realizing in the same breath that
no one will be convinced that this is the right
decision, yet, if you can't understand this
decision, I hope you can at least forgive me.

I am not the man I dared to be as a young lad. I
have failed my own name. I have smudged me with a
host of deplorable deeds, all dripping with lies
and arrogance. With even greater shame, I have
believed the very lies I've vomited. That stench
lingers where I trod and I have ran much, running
in place, splashing in stink, slipping on my
makers, my God, myself, my love, my friends.

My noteworthy accomplishments could be written
on a 3x5 index card, hidden beneath a stain of
selfishness. My resume, double-spaced, fills a
one-sided printers page. Interviews are sarcastic
set-ups for rejection. My passion pales in
comparison to experience. And a degree in Him
leaves you just as lost as you began. I never
intended to be well-known-versed-traveled-and-
wealthy, but I sure envisioned being somewhere
other than here!

I would rather feel anything than nothing, but
numbness has befallen on my heart. I pretend to
possess much love, just none to give. I reach
into my jar of faces and find a smile a day, but
like all things that come in a jar, once the seal

is broken, freshness deteriorates. My smile has soured. I have littered shards of me on a many of lives and land. Now to picking up those pieces of me, I am left with a bellowing question, "how do you put the puzzle of you together, when you don't even recognize the pieces?"

Defective. Defeated. Dejected. Disappointed. Desolate. Oh, Webster penned a definition to these adjectives, but those definitions are as vapor when they become the hell that swallows you. Nonetheless, as Barry sings, "it's only words, and words are all I have . . .", my ink begins to spill from what is left of a deflated heart:

Mine eyes are bleeding out of the well of my soul,
My prayers are lost in the breeze.
My words stand up on the tip of my tongue as a wilted flower,
My grace is spilt upon my sleeves.

My heart has fallen over and drowned in the mud,
My hands tremble as the crashing of waves on the shore.
My stare has set on the sun in the west,
My pride perches as crumbles on the floor.

My feet are shod with the stench of yesterday,
My hope dissipates as swiftly as the morning fog.
My salvation is nailed to unseen tree,
My last breath whimpers for a forgiving God.

What is left of this miserable shell of a man has thought much of ending it all . . .
. . . and then I did.

my letter to God

One year ago today, served as the beginning to
the darkest month of my life. To save myself from
myself, I began to pedal a bicycle and as I pass
the eleventh thousand mile marker, I've witnessed
my tears and sweat drip away twenty eight percent
of who I was, searching for a boy I once knew.

Most days, I'm amazed that I'm alive.
The other days, I'm wondering why I still am.
Today finds me thankful I am.

I've never done such, as I've done today, but
instead of whispering a prayer, I wrote a letter
to God, realizing He'll read it before I even
jot it down. Nonetheless, I signed and sealed
it. Took a stamp from ma-n-pa's because why go
postal when they're free at your former home, and
wrote an address to where I think Heaven might
be - Asheville, NC - somewhere just beyond the
mountaintop, where the grandest tree stretches
its neck the farthest and kisses the bluest sky!

I wrote my letter on the fanciest of recycled,
organic paper, because I'm still in that phase
of life where I think the nicer the paper, the
more credible and poetic the words, but as I
began to place pen to paper, I could only bleed
one sentence before the tears began to smudge a
poured and broken heart in ink:

Dear God,
Thank you for loving me, when I don't even love
myself.
Sincerely,
a cracked clump of clay

thirteen months *Wednesday, September 7, 2011 at 9:01pm*

September seventh of twenty eleven marks the thirteen month anniversary of the day I wanted to die. The mere penning of those words scares the shit out of me, but it has been since I found my way to the bottom of who I was, that I believed I could pedal my way back out. I've written much over the course of this past month of what I've learned while swimming beneath the belly of fish, yet as my silence becomes a screaming whimper, I voted against my first draft and hath decided to limit my morbid musings to a minimum of four, maybe less.

I've learned that *"never"* is the strongest word in the English language. *"Never"* can kill a man, and this I am sure, although *"never"* failed in killing I, *"never's"* grip was tightening around my shoulders, and took thirty percent of who I was and spilt me all over pavement. When she said *"I do"* to him, she said *"never"* to me. Never will I smell her smell. Never will I hold her hand. Never will I hear her laugh.

"Never" hums to a certain cadence of finality, a sister synonym of death, but being alive, it snatches away hope. The reality is, she chose *"never"* for me, leaving me helpless, hopeless, defense-less. When *"never"* occurs, when your mind and heart breaks, you learn that nobody sees things quite the way you do; you learn that nobody cares as much about you as you do . . . but you can't help longingly hoping that maybe someday, someone will.

(break)

I arrived in Asheville with a box to bury. Said box, seated passenger style, buckled in with plenty of leg room, vents angled strategically, held her, her memory, our memories. Much emotion, laughter to tears to middle fingers to pointers shared my journey. Weary from marring myself with guilt, shame, regret, and questions that will never be answered, I longed for rest, and thus I prayed the only prayer I could manage, *"Lord, lie at my back. My futures ahead of me, the tomb behind. Help me rest"*.

For the first time in months, I rested!

I dug a hole, placed years in the ground, watered it with tears, and laid dirt on top of a purple elephant. I've learned that it will always hurt - *because love will hurt until eternity begins*, but in retrospect, that hurt reminds me that I'm still alive. That I know what love is. That I've been there, I've done that, and I can't wait to do it again.

help me forget *Saturday, September 17, 2011 at 11:48pm*

. . . as I have penned, in times past,
concerning the subjects of which I write: I spy
saints, I stalk sinners, I copy conversations,
I mimic masks, I trace transactions. I listen
intently, I stare obnoxiously, I assume
intentions, I speculate reasons, I question
antics. I trod tearfully, I sit specifically, I
write alone. My notes, my musings, my rantings,
are merely receipts of stolen souls imprinted
in my mind and branded on my heart. Much of
my writings have been labeled "broken" or as
"readings for the misfits". I smirk at both
because we all have flaws tucked under our skirts
that only God and you can see, but it's so much
easier to slap a label on someone else's pain.

Nonetheless, the following four paragraphs, four
stories are intertwined with a binding thread
of pleading to forget their pasts. From child
abuse, to addiction and suicide; from losing it
all to a broken heart. Yearning (or learning)
to forget - I've been there, I'm there now, so
maybe this is mine own scream, but I'm certain,
many of you have been there as well, in one of
these sentences, in one of these paragraphs, in
this writing . . . and thus, that's me simply
whispering to you - *you're not alone!*

She makes wings out of cardboard and string
She jumps from her bed and makes believe
He hears a knock on the floor and he swings
She won't dream anymore after he leaves
But she'll pray to God - help me forget

(Stop)

He wasn't always like this - it started with just one
Now he's staring at his hands, pleading what have I done
He hears a knock on the door and he lays down
Puts a gun inside his head after loading one round
And prays to God to forget

(Stop)

The pieces are tattered and torn
The apple on the desk of being someone's worn
From being the man who sold the breeze
To scavenging puzzle pieces on his knees
He prays to God - help me forget

(Stop)

The color is gone and my heart has not won
I struggle to love and look into the sun
But you came and knocked on my door
And I wonder if you . . .
Will you help me forget?

my chance to say

. . . to have that opportunity to confront our
accuser, our broken heart, our shattered soul,
our worn will, our forsaken mind . . . to look
into the eyes of the soulless and the heart of
deceit . . . to say, *"do you see what you've done
to me - do you feel anything? - because I can't -
because of you!"*

Poor me!
Words fall out of my mouth like teeth;
few, with gaps in between.

I blame all those I hate, but name no names.
Perhaps they're written in my scars,
(for) someone stole my chance to say.

Poor me!
Left here dreaming on this bed;
your face, every scene inside this head.
When I dream, I scream in sorrow;
when I wake, all remains unholy hollow
(because) someone stole my chance to say.

. . . you hurt me, you made me cry -
see my scars - (right here) you're the reason
why.

You took what was rightfully mine
and left with a silent sway.
You didn't use words either;
but you stole my chance to say.

Poor me!
See you right back here tomorrow;
where words are scars and life is borrowed!

a left past worry Sunday, October 30, 2011 at 6:06pm

You do not sleep. It is a pretend rest. You view
1:37, 2:42, 3:27, 4:34, 5:42, which then leads
to counting ceiling fan panes 'til you turn off
the alarm clock three minutes before it is set
to alarm at 6:00am. You toss, turn, twist sheets
into knots, talk to shadows, and tally 'if's'.

You lie in this present darkness, worrying, but
not about toothpaste brands, correct calorie
counts, or Sophie's choice.

This is where worry dreams big. Where worry is
raw, with skin so real. Where food rots in your
gut. Where you can run away a boy or walk home a
man. Where prayers become bartered pleas - 'Lord,
if you get me out of this, I will never _____.'
Where you begin to doubt even your doubts.

It is about the hypotheticals - why did I this,
why didn't I that? I should have, I shouldn't
have. I could have, I couldn't. If only. What if?
Why?

You sit on the toilet and push. Nothing. You
use two fingers and heave. Nothing. Even your
body hates you. Something you use to be able to
control becomes an uncontrollable created chaos
in your mind. You wish to cry, to scream, for
someone to hear, for someone to share. Nothing.
No one. This is your created hell. Your mess, you
made.

You smile. You hide it well. Your mom, your
dad, your spouse, your boss, your associates,

oblivious. You put one foot in front of the other.
You perform the most mundane to perfection.
One day at a time. One hour at a time. One second
at a time.

You can't relax. You can't breathe. You're
everything to everyone and if you pause for even
a moment, you may tip over and spill all you
disguise! You can't lose yourself. You can't
compromise. You can't rewind. You've built this
lie on sinking sand. And you'll only rest when
you return.

And once again, tonight dawns . . .

on the right past worry *Monday, October 31, 2011 at 5:35pm*

. . . to every left, there is a right. This is the right to the left past worry.

You sleep. You rest. There are five ceiling fan panes. You know this because you've made it. You made it where worries wane and you win. Where worry hides behind a veil of forgetting to appear or where your fear appears and you decide to walk hand-in-hand with it. Where you realize fragments are easier to handle than figments. Where regardless of outcome, regardless of judgments, regardless of you, life happens.

Yes, it's going to hurt. You're going to cry. You're going to disappoint. You're going to choose poorly. But you're going to survive. You're going to smile. You're going to laugh. You're going to turn around and see the mountaintops of all the valleys you've conquered. And ooooh, it's going to be beautiful! A beautiful uh-oh. A beautiful rain. A beautiful worry.

my world around you *Tuesday, November 8, 2011 at 2:36pm*

I have been in love.
I have lost that which I was in love with.
I have wasted much mourning that which was lost
and loved.
I have lost me.
I have hurt many because I was lost and missing
and searching.

It is not what she built in me - it is what she
knocked down.

I miss that the most.

a boy who loved a girl

All it takes to cripple a heart like mine is a sound, a smell, a laugh, a name . . . a day alike today.

This is the story of a boy who loved a girl.

'Boy', she would pronounce with two syllables and 'Crusaders', upon a scream, sounded more like 'Gators'. I wrote them all down and crammed them into my tupper-ware three-drawer file cabinet. She, who would call her shower time, 'shopping in the hower' and lightning bugs on top of that mountain, 'litterbugs'. She, who never wrote me a poem but carved her Rushmore into the back of my eyelids.

A Broken Boy lives in those drawers. A Broken Boy who didn't want to let go. Call it fear, the unknown. Death.

I had a dream about her seven nights back. She was gone by the time I awoke. I thought if I could remember all the smiles, the smallest of details, she would stay. I thought we would last forever. She told me we would.

She lied.

a boy meets girl *Sunday, November 27, 2011 at 3:54pm*

. . . in my attempt to heal, to put square puzzle
pieces into an empty hole of a heart, I write!
I write to stay alive most days . . . I write
to release the floodgates of tears behind these
eyes! I've learned that someone's pain doesn't
have to make sense. That pain doesn't have to be
justified. That pain comes like people, in all
different shapes and sizes, and tolerance has
a broad definition. Maybe I'm not that strong,
maybe I can't take no more! Maybe I can move that
mountain, but today, I can't even lift my eyes.

Below is just another teardrop of my heart.
Another attempt to lift my eyes . . .

. . . this is a story of a boy meets girl,
two hearts bursting into three . . .
. . . and it ends with a bride and groom
becoming one 'neath our willow tree.

. . . this is a story of a bride in white
dancing on her wedding day;
of a boy-to-be picking up the pieces
when she went away.

. . . this is a story of a boy meets girl
who messes up everything . . .
. . . and it ends with a bride in white
wearing another's ring.

. . . this is a story of that boy-to-be
surviving on her wedding day;
of a heart that was and is bleeding,
'i wish you'd stay'.

she smiled at me *Sunday, December 11, 2011 at 8:30pm*

. . . it happens in all of our lives - whether
thru eye contact, a smile while riding an
escalator, a brushing of shoulders in a crowded
mall, or while waiting in a checkout line - when
time allows a stranger to become more than a
stranger for a fleeting moment.

We were taught as lads to believe that
fairy-tales do occur; that cupid, that love, can
strike, not only at midnight, but at any moment,
of any day, in any circumstance. Thus, we crave
that love that defies limits and transposes what
we already grasp! Wonderings know no bounds,
which offers a most bountiful musing below:

Dear beautiful ghost who smiled at me in the
checkout line,

I think we could make an 'us'.
I have an empty space, here and there,
with walls white as snow,
where we could paint countless, colorless
memories.

I have few possessions, aside from two cats,
but you might fancy my poetry
and I might like your baggage.

We could fall into each other
and note how grass on the other side,
is still just . . . grass.

. . . oh well,
the smile was nice.
Thank you.

nine syllables *Wednesday, January 11, 2012 at 5:15pm*

Peering down upon death two hundred forty five
feet below, at seventy-five miles per hour, only
four seconds separates death from life. The
somber distinction of *"where more suicides occur
than anywhere else in the world"* is smothered in
the fog lifting above the bay and on any given
week, throughout any given year, half a person
dies here.

Every two weeks, a whole!

(break)

I have yet to stand on the Golden Gate Bridge.
I have yet to cross the Mississippi in my
travels.
I have yet to attempt a suicide.
But.

(break)

Marking the page of which I did read last, a
postcard with a picture of the Golden Gate
Bridge looms. I often find myself staring so
intently into the picture that I begin to see my
reflection staring back at me. I get lost in the
'goodbyes' that have been said on that bridge. In
the hope unheld. In the scene of seen last.

Why did they jump? Why did they give up?
Why did they stop believing? Who broke the camels
back?
Who's the Juliet and where is Romeo?

(break)

It seemed to me that there was nothing more I could ask of life. Or nothing more I wanted. That I might take a deep, sweet, final breath, leap and die. I found it impossible to enjoy seeing love and thus I consoled myself with damning life.

(break)

"Coward". "Selfish". Two words used to describe those that succeed in suicide. And yet when I think of them, their lives, their hurts, their legacies and testimonies, I think of the word "brave". Maybe the "bravest of the brave". We all fear death. But to them, they did the one thing I couldn't. The one thing the majority couldn't. The one thing that can't be controlled and tamed it. Grasped it and decided its own fate instead of it thwarting theirs.

This isn't to glorify their success, but to magnify how deep the pain, the hurt, the tears flowed.

How death was peace, and living was hell.
How being alone in the ground, in a box, outweighed being alone in a crowd.
How leaping from a bridge was more freeing than being bound and gagged by the past.
How breaking every bone in your body upon impact was relief compared to a breaking heart, a broken mind!

(break)

My mountain: tis peculiar how one can be the greatest joy to another, and yet the profoundest misery to I.

(break)

I know no one that has leapt from the Golden Gate Bridge. However, I do tend to believe if someone had told them *"you made a difference in my life"*, that just maybe instead of leaping, walking would have continued to suffice. The power of words. The power in knowing someone believes in you. That someone is cheering you on. That someone will not let go! *"You made a difference in my life"* - nine syllables separating life from death.

(break)

My phone was on silent. I didn't want to talk anyways. I was all out of words, but I was willing to listen and what greeted me in the form of a voicemail saved me from leaping that day.

In a hushed tone of a voice, I heard these words: *"I wanted to die but you told me you believed in me, that I mattered! That I was important. That I was loved. Thank you for a making a difference in my life."*

And to them, thank you for making the difference in my own.

I am a testament to those nine syllables. A testament to the encouragement that I'm not alone, we're not alone. That we all make a difference.

life-changing lipstick

My description of the stench, of which I was
greeted with upon entering after the ninth step,
twill be an oft-injustice. The aroma burnt your
eyes, inducing your eyes to squint and your
face to crawl together like a wave from your
chin to your forehead, meeting somewhere in the
middle. It was like a full chicken house on a
hundred degree day with a sixty seven percent
dew point. Tis the smell of maggots feasting on
live corpses. Of death refusing to do what it's
supposed to do - suck out life.

It took much restraint walking past each room not
rushing in to aid their deplorable condition.
You were reminded that the individual did
not count - their name lost in a file - now
known only by room number, bed number. Branded
insane. Unstable. A threat to society, even unto
themselves. You knew they were dying, that they
were going to die, if not already dead.

The rooms were white. From the ceiling, to the
floors. From the walls, to the corners. The
mattress was white. No sheets. No windows. No
mirrors. A blank canvas of nothingness. Even the
little girl in this room had lost her color,
fading from a pinkish human to a ghost white. And
as a lasting insult to the rainbow, even the food
forgot to add color to the nothingness - steamed
white rice. (Might as well been worms, in my
opinion.)

She was naked. She stared at the locked door I
stood behind. A caged bird, who had forgotten how
to sing. Whose song was stolen.

And I asked the same question you're thinking –
How? Why?

She arrived two weeks prior. Found on Second
Street. She had cuts on her palms. Burns on her
knees and hip, as if she was discarded as a
lit cigarette, tossed from a creeping minivan.
An expired driver's license was found in her
training bra. Authorities contacted her mother.
Her mother said she was a mistake nineteen years
ago.

It was shortly thereafter I learned that she use
to weigh one hundred and sixty pounds – that
her mother mocked her as 'fat' – that she found
a stranger who introduced her to addiction –
that that addiction emptied her of self-esteem,
self-worth, self-appreciation, self-interest,
self-respect, self-love – that to make her feel
something, anything, she cut herself and those
cuts emptied her of life.

That's when I asked one of nurses if she had any
lipstick in her purse.

That night, a used stick of dollar tree lipstick
accompanied her portion of steamed white rice.

I received a call the next day.

Scribbled in lipstick ink on that locked door,
she had written: 'thank you for making me want to
look in a mirror again'.

That lipstick had done something to make her an
individual again. That she was more than her
illness, her disease. That she was someone.

No longer a room number. A bed number. A brand
or label. At last, she could take an interest in
her, her appearance. That lipstick offered her a
chance at being a human again. A girl again.

Angela died that night.
She had the rubiest of red lips.

once upon a time Friday, May 11, 2012 at 12:39pm

Once upon a time, twas a king who ruled a grand
and glorious land. Amongst his subjects was the
court courier of whom was his utmost favourite
of persons. The council agreed, the pheasants
agreed, the land agreed - this old man's hand
could write the fairest of speeches, of books, of
sentences. The king would spend ample of hours
each day reading this courier's words with wonder
and amazement.

One day, a disheveled, homeless boy approached
the throne and before the king himself proclaimed
that he was the grandest writer in the land.
The court laughed in bewilderment at the young
lads proclamation, however, the king, who always
fancied a challenge, set forth a competition
between the two writers, confident his courier
would squelch the lad in an embarrassing defeat.
The rules were simple: both had one week to
write their greatest work, allowing for only one
page; both would present that work in the town
commons for all the land to hear; and that work
which provoked the sincerest of emotions would be
championed.

The seven days concluded. Both writers arrived
in the town commons, ready to prove their worth.
The land came - pheasants, vagabonds, strangers -
from the north, from the south, the east and the
west. From all the corners of this vast land they
came. Even the birds presented themselves.

When the sun had set, the king stepped forth
ordering the court courier to proceed with his
story-telling abilities. The courier cleared

his throat and began. Upon 'the end', the birds chirped, the crowd roared in approval and satisfaction! The king stood and applauded, exclaiming: "Ahhaaaaaaa!! My courier has written the greatest story ever told."

After the cheers lingered for what seemed like days, the crowd hushed. Tis now the challengers chance to defeat the kings choice. The homeless lad stepped forth, cleared his throat and said softly, "*the queen is dead.*"

The skies began to weep. Even the king.

mr. walton *Friday, February 8, 2013 at 9:29pm*

It hurts today worse than it did yesterday and
yesterday worse than all the other yesterdays.
I have found myself going to Mr. Walton's at
2am eastern, knowing I should be sleeping, yet
knowing if I spent another moment alone . . .

I've climbed this mountain till my legs feel like
oceans, and every God-forsaken moment, I'm just
running thru the motions.

I've tried smiling, crying . . .
Adopting, fostering . . .
Buying, selling . . .
Hoarding, donating . . .
Bicycling, writing . . .
Sucking-it-up, duking-it-out . . .

Even tried out God a few times . . .

Still hurts.

I've always been terrible at praying.
I forget. I daydream.
I fall asleep mid-sentence. I use run-on
sentences.
I babble. I mumble.
I talk too much. I get confused.
I re-arrange the A.C.T.S of prayer into CATS or
STAC or TACS.
I pray too little.
I don't understand it.
I don't even know what it does or doesn't do.
And you would think after getting a 4.0 in
Christianity 101 and reading Andrew Murray's

656 pages on prayer, I'd have an inkling of an idea . . .

BUT . . . I do not.

I remember just the other night, I prayed the most terrible prayer . . .

All I managed to whimper was - 'Hey God, it's me . . .'

And then I wept . . .

Tis all I could utter . . . I couldn't get anything else out.

I don't remember falling asleep but this morning, I woke up.

That terrible prayer I said last night was the grandest prayer I've prayed in a long time.

I'm a terrible pray-er, and God loves me so.

breaking the silence *Sunday, June 2, 2013 at 8:09pm*

'. . . has anyone ever told you how Stephen died?'

'He was hers for 8 years and 4 months.
and he loved her immeasurably.
Granted, his way of expressing that love was odd
or reserved - some of that was him and his own
insecurities
- some of that was due to the distance between
Tennessee and North Carolina
- some of that was her
- but when she fell asleep and he kissed her
goodnight thru the moon that shined on both of
them, she knew she was loved.'

'Anyway, Christmas morning of that last month
together, he awoke to a text message from her,
reading, "I love you. I hope this is our last
Christmas ever apart."
He responded, "I love you back. I'll make certain
it is." '

'He never heard from her again.'

'One week later, thru an expired Target Wedding
registry, he discovered she was engaged to be
married to another. Wedding date, Christmas day.'

'He was found clutching his cellphone, having
typed, "I wish you'd stayed"
- intended recipient: 242-286-#her.'

'He never pressed "*send*".'

'She still doesn't know she killed him.'

snails *Thursday, June 27, 2013 at 8:25pm*

. . . stashed and crumbled in a worn-brown
leather American Eagle wallet, this poem resided.

Originally penned in late August, eight days
before my first tattoo, I remember hoping such
would serve as a cup of coffee and awake my senses
to do all those things I one day wanted to do.

Umph . . . the frailty of words - twas a grand
illusion - actions do speak louder and when
peering down upon my snail-like pace towards
all that I should be, I am reminded that I've
allowed my circumstances to mold me, rather than
my character. I've hid and secluded myself. I've
been frustrated and defeated. Once-coming-true
dreams are now taunts. And you can't pedal enough
miles to forget.

My cheerleaders have dwindled to a nary few - tis
oh so hard to receive love when you don't see
anything to love! Thus, you push - and not just
away, but out and under, slamming the door on
them, hoping even to catch their finger in the
door-jam so they'll hurt too. But isn't it ironic
that just as the door slams, you pierce your ear
into the crease, hoping you hear them breathing
on the other side, so you know you're not alone?

(Break)

I once thought I had the ability to be an author.
Thus, I took my journals of poetry and essays
and short stories and began shopping them to
various publishing agencies. Needless to say, I
couldn't find a date to the prom. Rejection is

demoralizing. Rejection's best friend is doubt.
And doubt is the reason this caged bird isn't
singing.

(Break)

A few years have passed. A publisher has called
me once a week for over two years. I've yet to
answer his call. Until today . . .

(Break)

My best friend has not let me go. She has
hounded, begged, pleaded, for me to cease my
utterance of 'one day I will' and simply 'just do
it'. 'Let go', 'let the chips fall as they may'.
And so today, as I answered the phone, the
Bostonian voice on the other end of the line
raced through the words, *'Mr. Wolfe, before you
hang up, this is Barry from . . .'* I interrupted
and said, *'I know who you are and I'm not hanging
up - let's talk about my book - Beautiful
Sprinkled Speckled Spackled Snails . . .'*

(Break)

. . . "the one day I will" poem
I've heard "almost" this many times;
just an encouraging synonym for "you've failed
another time".

I've been a leaf, floated on every winds blow;
I've been a seed, tossed where no grass grows.

I've been a vacation, another's last resort;
I've loved a many, yet failed to court.

I've been left, and I've turned right;
I've gambled all in, and lost that fight.

I've been a ghost in my own town;
I've pedaled too far, and gained no ground.

I've cried "could've", and settled for
"should've";
I've grand intentions, and await for "would've".

I've been a statue, and dreamt of pigeons;
oh . . . when will I just do it, and quit my
wishin'?

(Break)

When will I publish my first book? *You're holding*
it!

When will I ask her to dance with me again?
When will I forgive myself?
When will I forgive her?
When will I begin picking up the pieces?
When will I say 'I'm sorry'?
When will I begin to let go?
One day I will . . .

conversation *Sunday, June 30, 2013*

Stephen . . . As I have even pondered this
journey you have embarked upon once again . . .
My heart has been fearful as your Mom and my
protective spirit of you. You know there with be
accolades and also those who will "rain on your
parade." In the past I have seen those storms
cause you great pain, disappointment, and defeat.
My encouragement for you is to keep your eyes on
The Lord and realize others will let you down but
not Him! You have to decide from whence you are
"called" and not waver. As you before have gotten
discouraged by the "rocks" others have thrown
your way and you quit and went and thrown "rocks"
at the sky . . . at the One who from whence your
strength to overcome could of come. I don't think
either of us can take another "knockout" round.
Make sure who is leading you - then lean on Him
and go for it. Do it with humility and Him - and
there may not be guaranteed success - but there
will be guaranteed accomplishment on what He
wants to accomplish through you. Sometimes our
efforts we find are to change others and in the
end we look back and realize . . . we are the
changed
Love you with all my heart
MOM

* * * * * * *

I am certain of the fight ahead . . .
rejection is a part of this snails story, as
is disappointment and disbelief. I yet to know
why God gave me this uncanny gift of crawling
into the lives of strangers and spilling their
secrets, even my own, yet my life and theirs,

are stories that must be shared. Not all will receive, not all will understand, but He does . . . even unto my own understanding, I do believe I grasp not, yet sometimes the best is perhaps what we understand least.

Only real risks test the reality of a belief . . . you never know how much you really believe anything until its truth or falsehood becomes a matter of life and death to you. My matter of life and death has evolved, not from a solitary moment, but a three year journal entry.

Calloused in all the right places, but many more places to be touched, I do not believe that I will not be hurt, but I do believe He'll continue to heal my hurts and those hurts that I speak of.

These efforts to change one more life began with my own and the certainty that such shall continue is delighted upon within.

Forward, fragile, this snail marches on . . . .
Thank you!!! Love you . . .
Your Son

outside your window *Tuesday, July 2, 2013*

Just outside your window, is a canister
with dyed-red sugar water, hanging from a
steel-likened twine, fastened to the underside
of the vinyl siding to your ceiling. The purpose
of such a decorative display is to grasp the
hummingbird's attention and beckon, 'feast here'.

Ever since I was young lad, I've watched my
pa climb the ladder to retrieve this canister
and refresh its contents. He's a professional
climbing that ladder - 28 years of watching him
ascend and descend those steps, his footing has
been sure, without accident.

However, just after my 28th birthday, my dad
was demoted to the minor leagues of step-ladder
climbing. He climbed those steps with zeal, with
purpose - the sugary water needed replaced,
and hence, as he latched on to that apparently
slippery canister, he lost his balance and came
tumbling overboard.

Oh, earth is not a respecter of persons, and
thus, instead of landing in a field of white,
fluffy marshmallows, his wrist valiantly
attempted to cushion the direct impact of the
hurdling 200 plus pounds swiftly approaching.
Valiancy does not equal victory, and so be it,
his ulna bone, which is connected to his forearm
bone, which is connected to his elbow bone,
became dislodged! The other 200 plus pounds of
my Pa bounced upon collision, concluding with a
kitten-esque whimper of a moan.

Pa did attempt to self-medicate the dislodging of
that precious ulna bone, yet ice is intended to
make any desired item cold, not whole. Thus, with
the nagging persistence of a devoted wife, my pa
trudged to the emergency room.

Radiographs revealed a perfect shattering of the
ulna - the 'ulnic' puzzle pieces within my pa's
wrist had landed a ten spot - no surgery to be
required.

Three days later, pa was brandishing an
illuminated-neon, flashing blue cast from the
palm of his hand to three inches above his elbow,
bringing out his bold brown eyes, like Hershey
kisses in a Hershey kisses cookie.

I tell you, ladies and gentlemen, boys and girls
of all ages gathered with their Sharpie's to sign
my pa's - my fifty plus year old dad's cast.
Twas, as if that broken bone was a magnet - that
that blue cast had a spell within that made
all who viewed such, reach out with love, with
sympathy, with concern, with compassion, without
judgment.

(break)

Corey has a four inch scar on his left forearm.

No cast. No bandage.

And tomorrow, Corey will, once again, trace that
scar with a razor blade, with the vastest of
hopes to bleed out a memory he can't forget.

I wonder if Corey will receive the same treatment
as my pa?

duck-duck-goose *Friday, July 12, 2013*

. . . tis like playing 'duck, duck, goose'. Or
'hide-and-go-seek'. You've got to exercise your
inner thighs, or else when it comes time to
play, you're gonna pee all over yourself. It's
the thrill of being goosed, of being found, of
being chased, that begins a stirring within your
loins, expressed by this tingling sensation in
your thighs, felt by the warming in the seat of
your britches. I am not ashamed - my three decade
old self versus a class of 'kindergardners' and
I'm the one raising my pointer finger towards the
sky, trying to garner the teachers attention, to
let me go pee. It's like checking your facebook
page thirty two times in a six minute span to
see if she threw you a 'like', or responded
to your message you know she read at 7:16pm,
four hours ago. It's like going out to eat, and
ordering a salad, knowing you have a lettuce
intolerance, and all the way home, you're having
to pinch your butt cheeks together because you
don't wear Pampers. It's her walking into the
room you're in and the goose-bumps start in your
pinky toe that forgot to grow with the rest of
your toes and travels to the northern most tip
of your stubble-bald head. It's standing in the
fro-yo line behind the two teenagers who can't
stop fondling every topping on the buffet,
when you just want the granola in the little
canister beside the cashier. It's that first cup
of coffee at the hotel resort that was served
today, but brewed last Thursday, and you're
burping the aftertaste on your first day back
to work. It's wearing brown and black together,
or navy on black, and pretending GQ told you it
was now acceptable in today's society. It's man

capri's (guilty). It's bikini's in size three
x. It's salsa on eggs (crazy wonderful). It's
saying 'I'm sorry'. It's Texas yeast rolls in
A1 sauce. It's ketchup in mashed potatoes. It's
guys in flip-flops, or Crocs. It's not having
receipt paper at the gas pump (if I wanted to
come inside, I wouldn't have paid out here). It's
dancing like a dervish and running along the
tide with your arms out like you're an airplane.
It's rolling up your pant legs because socks
make the outfit. It's sticking your finger in a
uncooperative blender, and turning it on. It's
UNC fans in denial. It's toilet papering your
own house, to make you feel like someone cares.
It's the cold sweat dripping off your eyelashes
when you realize 'uh-oh'. It's her walking away
without saying good-bye. It's loving without
anything returned. It's that child laid to rest
before her first birthday. It's the son who never
came home from war. It's the grandpa who plowed
into eternity sitting on his Deere. It's the life
one chose not to live, and shoved themselves into
forever.

Life . . . doesn't make sense and doesn't always
add up to the sum we want . . .

. . . but oh, the crazy, insane, awesomely
filled-thrill called life, where broken-ness
meets glue and the shattered glass of the
unknowns reflect the most beautiful you.

und

part two - poetry

unusual

I am unusual, you stare.
It is a curse,
a disease,
a tiresome burden,
and every day I anguish.
I slip a blade into a vein
searching for a release
from a pain you don't . . .
          you can't (want) to understand.

You laugh
and mock
and think you . . .
have been more blessed
. . . can carry my load.
but you are mistaken.

I, alone,
live
and suffer
and slip
and howl.

In me, there is a crying rage
and I can't tell what's crying -
whether my broken heart,
or my wounded mind?

trail of me

. . . in a dark night, my mind begins to see,
a shadow in the shade.
I hear voices whisper in my veins,
the god of comfort begins to fade.
I sink to the bottom of silence,
beneath the belly of the fish,
and there join in muted matrimony,
the "o" to a star's fallen wish.

. . . what's madness but too many nights with,
to being nights without!
I know the purity of pure despair,
it is birthed at beginnings doubt.
I am a saddled soldier,
winter swallows my footsteps;
trace the trail of me to there,
I gave you all I had left.

defeated boy

His eyes are precipitating out of the clear
solution of his soul.
His prayer is losing its leaves.
His words stand up on the tip of his tongue as a
wilted flower.
His grace is spilt upon his sleeves.

His heart has fallen over and drowned in the mud.
His hands tremble as the crashing of waves on the
shore.
His stare has set on the sun in the west.
His pride perches as crumbles on the floor.

His feet are shod with the stench of yesterday.
His hope dissipates as swiftly as the morning fog.
His salvation is nailed to an unseen tree.
His last breath whimpers for a forgiving God.

why

I cut to focus when my brain is swelling
I cut to visualize all I hold inside
I cut to feel when all is numb
I cut to smell the breath of all I hide

I cut to paint faces of the lost
I cut to carve lasting impressions
I cut to sculpt reminders of love
I cut to write I was here

I cut to cast away yesterday
I cut to wash away the stain
I cut to burn away all memory
I cut to blot away your name

I cut to bleed
I cut to scream
I cut to cry
I cut to forget

I cut to live
        (to stay alive)

garden

My arms are open wide
Have a look inside
Run your fingers over
Trace my reasons why

Thru the garden of carved love
Under the trees of innocent thieves
Smell the blooms of broken rooms
Dance on the sidewalks of outlined chalk
Wade in the waterfalls of stained stalls
Marvel at the statues of wordless blues
Linger on the benches of knotted lynches
Spy on the nests of sheltered pests
Swing wide the gates of forgotten fates
Pull up the weeds of unsown seeds
Skip the rocks of discarded socks
Spread out the blankets of silver droplets
Kick the dirt of my blue earth

Don't neglect
On your way out
To wash your hands
Of my silent shout

Because they're stained red
From all I've bled

down

Down to my last
Hands held high
Tear stained face
Closed eyes

Bowed head
Begin to pray
Scars cannot hide
Want to stay

Disappear with rage
Discover lost within
Disappoint love
Disease on my skin

Walk like an army
Strangers track dust
Lies disguised by man
Porcupine musk

From yesterday
Time to harm
Traced footsteps
Written on my arms

Tap my shoulder
Let your light shine
Hold my hand
Still have time

One unspoken word
Blade on the floor
Heart unlocked
Please open the door

blue fade red
for Lisa

The color blue,
disappearing into a puddle of red,
reminds my poor soul
just how precious is

                                life.

Enveloped in darkness,
emptied by fear,
eaten by regrets,
the song of my heart

                              beckons

me to escape
these concrete halls.
To trade stains
for scars,

                               I must

become something
I do not know.
Hand you my disguise;
trust the real me will

                              follow.

And pray He
understands . . .
forgives . . .
forgets.

blue china plate

I hold in my hand
Fragile as a feather
Held as loosely as sand

Would love to squeeze
A knife into my vein
To stop this maddening
This sick insane

Blue china plate
So much time and detail
If only someone would listen
I wouldn't go to hell

Would look to the stars
Waiting for one to wink
Life is like a vapor
Only one more blink

Blue china plate
I hold in my hand
You are all I have
I hope you understand

Blue china plate
Broken on the floor
Pieces of me found
When they open the front door

bride

Have you ever felt so tattered,
no one to patch the pain?
Step one: thread the needle or
no step: exposed vein.
Either step: slip a finger inside.
My love is open wide;
take a dip, my new bride.

My sleeves are stained red
from all the truth I dread.
I'm laying all my secrets aside
of why I'm empty inside.
Take my hand and say a vow
to notice if I live or die.

Your dress falls gently to the floor;
it's dancing gracefully in melody.
I peel back my skin
to watch my love's spilt tragedy.
I lie on the floor,
the thought of ending it all
creeps just outside the door.

Here inside this room,
hear me cry.
Here on this bed,
death draweth nigh.
Lay your head on this pillow,
close your eyes to this sin.
I try to look at you,
but can't stop what has been.

Bride is absent, a dress remains.
Empty bed, all the sheets are stained.
All is quiet, except for the drop of the blade;
a patchless, frayed serenade.

bathtub

just enough water
so that when
i lay flat,
the water rushes
over my eyes
and peaks at
my nostrils.

if only
my mind would
allow me to
dive an inch
deeper,
i'd wash my face
of all the
disgrace.

(I cross my arms across my chest,
soon to fall asleep in peaceful rest.
Allow the water to breach my head,
in three more minutes, I'll be dead.)

falling

Staring out my window,
from the 13th floor balcony,
I reach for a star.
It pricks my fingertip
          (and I wonder) -

star-light, star-bright,
defeated by a night so black,
how did you ever learn to scream back?

Do you sparkle?
Do you burn?
Do you wish?
Do you yearn?

Is it a worthy confession
to attempt to disobey your calling,
because the Hall of Stars
is littered with busts of the falling?

The midnight sky lies to this inner earth;
for the fallen here lay quietly in the dirt.

gust

the past:
           fragments of stolen innocence.
      lie,
      rot,
      sleep,
      in the dark,
      at the bottom
      of an empty
      well of pride.

the blade:
           fragments of slippery steel.
      break,
      steal,
      mask,
      in silent action,
      a shadow shelter
      nailed up out
      of darkest longing

the puddle:
           fragments of spilt blueberries.
      cry,
      moan,
      drip,
      in starry union
      to the truth
      of a broken
      gust of god.

weeping willow

Day is at rest
Night perches out its chest

Beauty from afar
More sacred in the dark
Climb the sycamore
Sit atop the magnolia
While willow weeps

Upside down leaves
Straining for oxygen
Preying on an invisible supply
Of waters abundance
While willow weeps

Branches are knotted
Roots are penetrated
An internal parasite
Cripples the heart
While willow weeps

Faded flowers fall
Stained sap invades
Drips of dew
Litter the dust
While willow weeps

Bruised to used
Bark to scars
Fruit bears none
Pliable to liable
While willow weeps

Rigid to tender
Grandeur to slender
Plays tag with earth
Stretches towards heaven
While willow weeps

Marvel at her appearance
Shrug at her demise
Leave her bleeding in her bed
Keep this scene inside your head
Willow is now dead

impressions

"Impressions create character."

I'm creating character.
Acting out a screenplay,
on the stage of my arms.

My blade, the puppet.
My hand, the string.
My brain, the author.

Impressions of love, scream each scene.
Impromptu dialogue, deems of release.
Impotent vein, empty of air.

Pull the velvet, no standing ovation.
Take a bow to a silent army:
me,
myself
and
God makes three.

bruise

Blind bruise
Scream to use
Half the rainbow
Blow by blow
Spread red
Tuck in bed
Flow blue
Here's to you
Turn yellow
So shallow
Fade black
Drift back
Next time around
Broken clown

bird

On dented knee, here's to you,
a story of a bird's devotion blew.

A call to fly was never true,
only time to suffer a fatal bruise.

High aloft this silly tree,
a promise of tomorrow twill never be.

Stuck in rewind in this fleshy nest,
one more round of dreamless rest.

Drop from the branches leaves lost,
puddles on the ground as a violent frost.

Wind walks by to bid farewell,
only to find a bird's hollow shell.

clean too

I wash my hands a thousand times;
the blood still remains.
My innocence lost
beyond the bow of rain.

Why must your smell linger,
your touch crawl my skin?
Why must your purity
stain all that lies within?

I close my eyes -
your etched on that sacred place.
Every tear,
a trace of your face.

I hearted you,
you haunt me.

Porcelain no shade of white;
mirror beholds a ghost staring back.
Ghosts can't see red;
all fades to black

bury

bury all
my sins,
all my
secrets,
deep within
my skin.

six feet shallow,
the cry
within
my heart.

my tears
soften the soil
where my
memory
will rest.

here's to you:
three inches.
spend a night
in my shoes,
nothing left
to prove.

the moment before

I ask my God for forgiveness
I write love on my arms
I cut myself to bleed
                        a sweet crimson release
I damn my soul
I flush my dreams
I gnash my teeth
                        on the hollow of my soul
I hide my masks
I swallow my pride
I pour my tears on the floor
        trickling down from an everlasting Stream

I scream at the darkness
I argue with trees
I crawl in shame
            crawling pass the crowd to a cross

I justify my insanity
I drown in lost love
I reach for the Light
                            that seals my pardon
I squeeze crazy from my veins
I wave goodbye
I leap into the abyss
                    leaping only to be caught
                    by a landslide of Love

            a love that wouldn't let go
unconditional
separated not by life or by death

                            I am at rest

every note, a song

. . . every note, a song.
. . . every word, an exclamation.
. . . every comma, an extension.

. . . every tree, a forest.
. . . every cloud, a sky.
. . . every rainbow, a promise.

. . . every doubt, a reason.
. . . every failure, a success.
. . . every success, a blessing.

. . . every second, a chance.
. . . every prayer, an answer.
. . . every dream, a hope.

. . . every lie, a truth.
. . . every scar, a face.
. . . every butterfly, a change.

. . . every love, an object.
. . . every life, a gift.
. . . every person, an image.

. . . every color, an expression.
. . . every circle, a hole.
. . . every shadow, a light.

. . . every name, a legacy.
. . . every death, a birth.
. . . every tear, a waterfall.
. . . every August, a September.
. . . and everything ever lost,
an opportunity to be found.

frozen

take me where time stands still
to a dream too hard to believe

just you and me
where a cloud lingers when we breathe

the weight of yesterday beneath our feet
if we can just be free
i want you to sit with me
the weight of yesterday beneath our feet

dreams do come true
it's the falling asleep that haunts
night is waiting
but you linger
just you and me
where a cloud lingers when we breathe

the weight of yesterday beneath our feet
if we can just be free
i need you to sit with me
the weight of yesterday beneath our feet

our eyes froze the world in time
we sat together and watched it melt
it was the only thing left to do

one by done

my hand is numb
from the weight i did hold
the curse of loves wilted flower
fallen and cold

you sit all alone
recounting all my sins
you name them one by one

oh it's dark
in this empty home
my eyes blurry
peering monsters in the shadows

i once needed you
and you let go
you sit all alone
recounting all my sins
you name them one by one

memories of us
an open atlas
me
who i'm gonna be
another chance
that girl and that first dance
i win
i win

and you
you still sit alone
recounting all my sins
you name them one by one
look around, all your friends are gone
oh, what did you win

foiled bow

I
In the failed grip of quietus,
I have not flinched or cried aloud.
Pinioned by cerebral hiatus,
my head is stained, but unbowed.

II
Beyond these walls of rage and wrath,
looms a quiet coil.
Trace my love in puddles path,
to the Silhouette's scheme unfoiled.

stars

My arms are my night sky -
connect the scars.

Peel the curtain,
expose the love carved.

Dip your finger
in my constellation of stars.

Wish upon a promise
to never be so far.

All of me is torn,
sad and shooting and worn.

Why did God ever pause
to wash His hands?

crystal

He tells me that he loves me
I call him my prince
(Devil with crystal eyes)

He makes crumbles of my heart
I trust him with my life
(Devil with crystal eyes)

He steals my innocence
I let him in my veins
(Devil with crystal eyes)

I wish I'd never greet him
Because I can't resist
Every time he whispers
Hold me in your arms

Mess is made
Blue red fades
Red fades black
(Devil smirks back)

Please let me go
I was never sold

Somebody rescue me
Save my weary soul

we make the deal

His words as smooth
as caramel upon my tongue.
Exchange our pooled blood,
for a folly flood
of life within a jar,
tossed to that space
between each star.

So high til it feels
like my heart
might drop;
drown me from
the inside out
to complete
this fables flop.

He grins,
the corners of his mouth
spray a deceitful drawl;
it's like riding a bike,
I won't let you fall.

The demons planned
an overnight stay;
stole my pretty away.

He didn't let me fall;
for you can't fall
when you crawl
to the place where
darkness meets
and
flames greet.

bloody shepherd

they went inside
each to their assigned pew
where walls are formed

tucked away into a terrible space
where monsters are born

enclosed by plaster lies
where belief grows cold

feasting on infested scraps
where crumbs litter the mold

question after question arise
answers only to despise

respect
expect
require
acquire

the tangled web of the shepherd
dismembering his own horde

demons

Demons hide in dark corners. Dark corners
can be harmful. In the light, you're more secure.
You have no need of darkness; in the dark
obsessions grow. One glimpse, a slip occurs.

In solitude, you cut. Your vein abandoned
before your eyes, in puddles of blue, where love
once loomed.
Thus, night will weep tears upon your hollow
soul;
drowning, wandering in a sea of swollen gloom.

Keep open your eyes for painted fingertips.
We all have weapons to self-conceal;
yet one raised hand is required
to blind the demon of all that's real.

daisy

I've seen a girl with borrowed eyes,
tiptoeing through a field of daisy lies.
Lazy days of picnics and love,
saddled to the back of an unwilling dove.
Scratch the bark of that poisonous oak,
etched for the tears of rain to cloak.
Mingle kisses with the stars,
drown in the serenade of seeping scars.
Sun waves goodbye to grass so black,
passion ablaze as the moon smirks back.

I've seen a girl with blotted eyes,
daisy petals resting by her side.

secrets

secrets are safe with no one
not even that secret carved in the back of your
knee
that place where only you
and God can see

secrets rot in that abyss
maggots feast on veins
and ooze with smiles
smiles of pure rebellion

my sleeves are stained red
from drops of secrets bled
wring out reasons of shame
to stain the hands of blame

dance on the secrets
of muted reflection
sway to future waves
tiptoe on hallowed ground
past skeletons
past frozen oceans
past butter-flys
past beds so empty

ten feet off the ground
to six feet under
secrets bury coils
with just one feather

draw

If ever God made a mistake, tis you!
If ever skin was a waste, tis you!

Keep smiling . . .
Keep swaying your hips . . .
Keep pretending.

You think you own me
but I have your picture.

And
I'll keep that picture alive
in my nightmares,
in my wishes,
in my intentions,
as I dig you a hole.

Toy with my pride,
I'll toy with your soul.

Just a stained glass mom,
drenched in a cataract
of a sticky (viscous) bee balm.

And I'll wave goodbye with a smile,
as you stare into my eyes,
gasping for air,
choking on the earth
I place on your face.

You should've known me
and what I'd do to you.

Enjoy breathing through a straw -
you started the counting:
one, two, three, draw.

speak

No lights
No sound
A choking calm in the air
I reach into the drawer
Feeling for what I know is there

I try to block the rage
I try to escape the hate
Do I not deserve
A more bittersweet fate

These walls must be talking
It's swelling my brain
My hand is trembling
These scars are not in vain

I bite on the corner of my lip

I slip

The blade hides within my skin
Blood drips off my fingertips
Layers of me exposed

I dare you to take a dip

My arms
My scars
This is my world
My shelter in the rain
You stand just outside the door
Please help me
Please
Please speak my pain

eyes

Eyes tell the truth
Eyes craft stories untold
Eyes hold secrets
Eyes watch lies unfold

I stared into her eyes
    as into a thousand suns
    and
Am blinded by fear
    from a dark chocolate dreamy fun

Hopelessly
    her eyes promise forever
Cautiously
    her eyes craft a pretend endeavor

Her eyes flatter with vows
    of only me
But are they hollow
    have I made them make believe

I cannot find the answer
    only a doubt of totality
    only a diagram of today
    only a dream of tomorrow

Her eyes screamed words
    but are they truth or fairy fables
To be discerned
    I wonder if even she is able

truth

Some days I think
my mind slips.
I argue with trees,

                              praying

prayers that seem
to go unanswered;
even unheard.
Am I so shallow

                         to believe

that this is pointless,
that the way I perceive Him
is through the lies I watched
in the pew?

                       The truth

is hidden.
I know I have to go out
and seek it,
but truth

                             can be

like a prodigal –
not always where it should be;
once was lost
but now must be

                          found.

masks

I wear many masks!
Some way too despicable
to fit the smile
super-glued to the back of them.
                                        I

keep a fresh stash in a box
called my heart.
It's filthy in there -
tainted with looks, I
                              don't

allow anyone to see.
Not that anyone cares
to go looking,
Not even you . . .
Who really wants to
                              know

what bothers me?

Too stuck up your own agenda
to see I'm about to wave goodbye!

Today, I open
my precious little box
one more time.
If only I could find
the mask labeled
the real
                              me.

could've (should've)

I could've been a boy
I could've been a girl
I could've been bald
or had golden curls

I could've been made for the big time
My name could've littered the sky
I could've had eyes as diamonds
My picture could've mesmerized

They all could've said I had potential
All the world could've known my name
They all could've said I'd be a star
I could've been living in fame

I could've practiced my autograph
Been recognized from sea to sea
I could've cured cancer
Been a celebrity

My voice could've answered
nightly curtain calls
I could've walked the red carpet
My bust hollowed in the Halls

I could've lived in Hollywood
or just down the street
I could've made beautiful music
with my dancing feet

I could've brought you much joy
I could've shown you another way
I could've made you smile
Want to wake up another day

I was beautifully crafted
Wonderfully formed
But you went and saw that doctor
and I was never born

waffles

day
is
done,
tear
stained
face.
dim
the
lights,
hate
this
place.

two
o'clock,
all
felt
up.
haunt
my
dreams,
no
breakfast
waffles
with
syrup.

lay me down, Lord, my soul to keep.
better
yet,
do
not
let
me
fall
asleep.

starlight, starbright

She wipes the blackened streak
from her flushed cheeks
She is broken
scattered in the wind
Wave the white flag
on the love that she has won

Oh starlight
starbright
Don't you cry
We're gonna make it home –
Home where we belong

She sleeps on stained sheets
Prays her soul to keep
She is afraid
Rest in a butterfly cocoon
Shed a dead skin
on a love that she can't win

Oh starlight
starbright
Don't you cry
We're gonna make it home –
Home where we belong

revelry

It seems unbelievable
That half a dozen letters
Strategically arranged
Could say so much

My revelry would be to -
Paint in on every wall
Scream it in to every well
Carve it into every tree
Notch it into every bench
Melt it into every precious metal
Shout it standing in the valley
Letting the mountains echo back
Those separate five letters

My revelry would be to -
Teach the birds to sing it
Teach the fish to drink it
Teach the wind to breathe it
Teach the sun to shine it
Teach the skies to rain it
Teach the human that nothing
Nothing compares to the madness
of You

My revelry would be to -
Forget the other 21 letters
Set fire, the books that I've read
Garbage, the poems I've written
Blot, the lips of spoken word
Flush, even the numbers

To greet one another with your name
To whisper good-night with your name

My lasting cadence upon the hearts of kindred
Rests on the shoulders
Of those five letters

And I'll sail to the other world with your name
on My lips
All their questions will be answered with your
Name
The sinner, the saint, the demon, the angel
The judge will sentence me to proclaiming it
Endlessly

the potter's ocean

Looked for a place
to bury my face.
Found the ocean,
drowned in grace.

Looked for a way
to die today.
Found the Potter,
returned to clay.

prodigal

With folded hands, you'll bow and pray;
though he deny them, continue your stay.
He will resist, wage war, rebel;
yet while resisting, longs to be held.

The path chosen tempts the lonely;
a prodigal buried in winter only.
He will awake, repent, and hear;
the melting of a stone by prayers and tears.

parade

I'm not sure what shattered my will
Why can't broken hearts be filled
I've carved love into my arms to make it go away
but the stars keep crying on my display

And as I sit here tonight holding this blade
I'm not so sure I can continue living this parade
My scars speak of an innocence betrayed
and I can't stop the stars from crying on my
display

Blood is the release pulsating through my veins
It's the mask of a fool running from the pain
If only a cut could answer for the bouquet
resting under the stars crying on my display

fear of commitment

I love you with all my heart . . .
I love being with you . . .
I love whom you've made me into . . .
it's just —

forever is a really long time.

full

My mind is full of pills and stories
From the light of slipping in and out
My eyes are full of endless stories
Yet no words to pen to my silent shout

You give me a number
And strap me to a bed
Let's all count to ten
One two I wish I was dead

I didn't choose this
It's a mental disease
And I'm not having a relapse
I'm just in the midst of making crazy

But you don't get me
You only hear the sound of the drip
There's so much more to me
Beyond all my secret slips

(break)

I would've asked you for a favor
To save me from myself
But I didn't want to interrupt you
From playing with yourself

games

. . . it's only a game
until you find someone
who plays the game
better than I -
and I don't know
if I'm mad
or if I just
want to
cry
or
die!

dust

My arms are tried and true,
from years of buy and sell.
My eyes have seen the glory;
pull up my sleeves for show and tell.

Pain is a beautiful option,
but I'm bored with that as well.
I need another escape - another release,
please, save me from myself.

The moon is made of chrome;
my skin is made of dust.
Puddles are the world in which I hide,
no one lives here I can trust.

So let this be my plea;
the flower pinned to my lapel.
I need somebody to listen -
please, save me from myself.

him

a single thread woven throughout mankind
connects us all
that thread knotting at His feet
just where I landed with my fall

after wiping the dust and sand from my eyes
there they were
two feet just as dirty as I
my tears could've washed them clean
if only this was a different scene

be sure your sins will find you out
here my sin has lead me to this place
only his feet hid my shame
only his hand I saw as I lifted my face

shattered my dreams
naked my skin
abandoned my heart
exposed my sin

angry the crowd
missing my lover
stained my cheeks
his feet my only cover

coffin

bury all your sins
all your secrets
all your time lost
bury them six feet under
the hate
within my heart

may my tears
soften the soil
where your memory
will rest

you are selfish
you are proud
you are all
I never wanted

my hands are held high
I take back all that was yours
I know you're laughing
but read between the lines
I'm about to let this fly

I'm destined to be
better than you
you stole my heart
you stole my innocence
I stole your mind

I've been through the valley
I've seen the night sky
I've waited for truth
and truth finds me
without you

tag

I fear the voices inside my head,
floating in the wind.
They laugh at me.
They mock me,
whisper and stalk me
and chase me.

I've yet to realize,
they can't chase me
if I stop running.

streak

Sometimes I feel like dying naked.
Sometimes I feel impressed to undress -
to bare my scars before your invisible eyes,
to hang on display my last breath,
to sway as a pendulum,
to be your curriculum
on what happens when you live in there and never
come out to stare.

winkle

dead diamond glitter
twinkle in my eye
i'm all out of tears
the waves forge a lie

the dam begins to crumble
with each floating second
come back from the ledge
may your soul be awakened

i can see you slipping
no longer found
i can see you starting to break
no longer bound

idol

despoil: to strip of value
disguised disgustingly
edited effeminately
stripped sacrilegiously
preserved poorly
organized ornately
idolized ignorantly
loved legislatively

what *church* has done to God.

clown

In the morning, after the rain
and the humidity rises,
Lisa awakes and disguises.

Off with the frown
and down with the sleeves,
truth is treated as she turns to leave.

Turns the key
on a truth not told,
just another day living as fool's gold.

barter

The rain pours, the love streams.
The lion roars, the demons scheme.

Imagining what it feels like to be free,
instead of caged, broken, and lonely.

Stuck in a corner for your pity;
death begins to look oh so pretty.

A gentle glide from a beloved friend
will give me peace in the end.

With a bowed head and folded hands,
God grant me a second chance.

To cast my cares at your feet –
in exchange, give me back
the real me.

gray

a stain
so pure
written on my arms
a path of lonely destruction
questioning me with white lies of charm

a fear
so bold
walks back to obsess
a fantasy of bitter freedom
losing me within black holes of progress

a life
so old
wasted on gazing back
a hell of my procrastination
killing me softly in white and black

hollywood

I do it to punish myself;
to remind myself why I hide.
I seek out those whom never notice;
to mock them when they find.
I hear their laughter, no screaming allowed;
from the red carpet to the closet,
it's easier to be alone than in a crowd.

slippery

hello my friend
it is time again
it is time again to slip
it is time again to slip inside
for I have slipped once more
and I fear if I slip again
I will never slip again

we all want to belong to someone

I must write while my ego is altered
Otherwise my words foundation will crack and
falter

Balanced between the sun and the moon
Swings the meaning of right and wrong
Forsake conviction
When all I want is to belong

Go to the alter and confess all your sins
Tap the shepherd as he ruins

In my own blue (s)hell
Where all is feared

Fool the priest
Who lead me here

scarecrow

You've made me a scarecrow –
hung and hollow.
I've traveled so far
to be six feet shallow.

My souls been stuffed with straw.
I'm bursting at the seams
to itch the flea
that gnaws on my mind
and sifts on my skin.

There's no rest in this field.
My fear is your appeal.
To stand in attention,
to quietly grieve.
If I could walk,
I would leave.

disappointment

before the phone landed,
i heard the sound of my father's tears.
my last words had made him cry.
i cried because i had made him cry.
i will not forgive myself;
for i am the boy who made my daddy cry.

mine

roll up your sleeve and i'll roll up mine
together we can see all i hide
don't leave me alone at this time
for i'm afraid of what we'll find

i know i will find a hole
within the hollow of my soul
i have filled this void with mock memories
where my innocence was stole

i know i will find a break
within the thump of my heart
i have sealed this fault with stained smiles
where my world was torn apart

i know i will find a scar
within the color of my skin
i have written love with idolum ink
where my death was poised to win

hold my hand and walk my hill
to a place called grace and time
and i'll learn to forgive myself
(even him) who had no right
to take this soul that is rightfully mine

vacation

Where did Stephen go?
They say he lost his mind
I think he lost his soul

He lost his passion
He lost his pride
Sits alone with no rhyme
And reason has died

His cup is broken
The world is empty and dry
He waits and wonders
How long will it take to die

Summer fell past winter
And tears fell in spring
Her hands choke his north
As she slips on another's ring

Where did Stephen go?
He's lost but found
We think he's given up
But Stephen isn't in the ground

(_____)

afraid of emptiness (detachment), as I am,
my soul attaches (clings) to "things"
trying to create (preserve) . . .
. . . express (merit) . . .
. . . find (lose) . . .
. . . belong . . .
(to) something neither confessional nor public
yet, rather a place of strangled truth and
drowned grace!

119

glass jar

as she sits on the edge of her bed and cries
she closes her eyes and pretends
she hears a knock on her door and reminds herself
it'll be over in minutes and lays downs

another night alone with a stranger in her bed
she'll count the money and he'll run
she closes her eyes and prays
she's trapped again in nightmares
but every time she realizes she's awake

are there any ears to hear her cries, her prayers
she should be loved but she is labeled
she closes her eyes and prays to forget
it's another night of forgetting fables

ignorance

here I lie forever
grief fills this grave
baptize me
wash it all away
drown me in water
forgive me with blood
whisper so long to never
where i am every day
you chose to ignore

sustain

blue blood flows thru my veins
it curls my hand into rock
it boils and blisters in my brain
it drips with a determined doubt

its got the preacher in me hiding
it pricks my painted heart
it stains my reflection shining
it floods this forgotten fate

it puddles on the bedroom floor
it drowns my happy ever after
it encourages this encore

it fans the flame
it blows kisses goodbye
it kicks sand in your face
as your red rose dies

moon

nail a flag on God's thumbnail
declare all is ours
and to each their own
yet to fall in the sea
and drown all alone

careless

i care little of your thought
it falls silently in my forest
years of love lie in waste
my heart shaded a dull rust

i care not that the holiest
pretend to be holier than i
but that they toy with my fate
with a moat in their own eye

i heed none that my cup of youth
runneth over with blood and tears
that the sting of one lie
has paralyzed all my remaining years

it's not that flowers do not bloom
or that the rivers have run dry
it was only my undoing
i shot the sun and murdered the sky

so do not weep for me
as you say your last amen's
i died long ago on a day i lived
to find she will not love me ever again

twin

I watch you live out the Gospel of Judas
Fulfill your role as Shakespeare's Brutus
Quote me verses and wash my feet
Kneel at the altar, pray with conceit
Sing a hymn and raise your hand
In "Jesus" name, take a stand
Forget to confess and who you profess
Meet death tonight, you failed to impress
Stand at the gate and hide your face
Keep your religion, I'll cling to grace

scraps

the sky is painted black tonight
the stars closed their shutters
and God blew out the moon

the trees stretch out their arms
the fly tap dances on my wall
and God was lonely so He exhaled

the kid from yesterday dropped a penny
the well eats his dream
and God builds a scarecrow

the world is a heap of broken things
the mirror never lies
and God plays with puppets

the handkerchief holds my hand
the clock steals the slipper
and God forgets to look

the moon moves to the left as God inhales
the scarecrow sings to the field of puppets
as God looks past my head and begins anew

true story

I was exhausted.
It wasn't worth getting out of bed.
And so I peed all over myself,
"I'll wipe it up later", I said.

Four hours passed,
before I chose to awake.
I stood and beheld,
the mess I did make.

While cleaning myself, I whispered this prayer -
"Lord, let my mansion be a hut,
before I must rely on others
to wipe my own butt."

siegen

part three – unfinished musings

I have always struggled with the *so-often-said-and-thought* phrase of describing a circumstance or tragedy as being the "will of God". In my most un-blasphemous opinion, within the churches and circles that I have gained *live and in color* knowledge, I have heard the words, "we must trust this or that as the 'will of God' ", yet if everything is as the "will of God", then we are but mere puppets on a string strung stage. God, the playwright, depicting, acting, and achieving as He pleases. Destroying homes and families, as He deems so. We, with anchors and chains about our wrists, entering and exiting the stage, portraying our lives before a critical cast and audience, for sheer amusements sake. All to be hugged and comforted, even believing, it is all - all the "will of God".

(my sole question then hinges on the phrase of "free will" . . .)

Nothing so irritates me more than the ignorance of a Christian, or the incapacity of an intelligent being thinking that God has His ever sovereign finger on the trigger, His hands on the wheel, His knife out of its sheath, His potion or poison ready to infect. Never do we know enough and more of God than to utter a senseless tragedy (a death) as being the will of God. My only comfort rests in knowing that as the bullet, that took my friends life, breathed air its last, my God's heart was the first of all heart's to break.

_____

Chosen with caution, handled with care – a
gift relegated to a simple card must be above
reproach – the card must evoke emotion, must
speak volumes, must display absoluteness. The
words must hug-a-face, must steal-a-breath, must
dry-a-tear. With the aforementioned serving as
the pinnacle to which all enveloped cardboard
doth strive – this card fails! However . . .

In a subtle bold print, my chosen theme for
this mother's day is stamped. Ten letters,
strategically scrambled into a word of the
utmost magnitude. Time, nor space, allows for
the details, yet for ten thousand, six hundred,
thirty one and a quarter days, you have been
making a difference in my mind, my heart, and my
soul.

You are loved beyond ink.

. . . this morning finds me flipping thru crusted
pages of where I've been. Drowning in my own
tears, I can pen: *I've been through the water,*
I've come out clean, but I'm still wet! Not
healed, still bandaged, and sudden movements drop
me to my knees, but I am not who I was.
He's still working on me . . .

. . . if only the contractor was on sight . . . .

He reminded me of a young Junior Pack (and for
those of you who never met or heard of Junior
Pack, he was my grandpa, my Pépa, the grandest
of men). A bit more hair, but same wiry frame,
old timers glasses, oxford shirt, with elastic in
the band of his chinos. Brown shoes, brown socks,

height on par with my eyes, smile wrinkles on the corner of his lips, creases of time on his forehead, veins easily seen on his hands, and a mischievous twinkle in his eyes.

I asked the most random question of the year upon paying for my purchase to this "Junior Pack", which led to a brief biographical exchange culminating with his fingerprint on my mind and heart. I ended my biography with uttering, *"I'd give anything to be here . . . to live out my passion . . . to be where I truly want to be!"* As if I was talking to my own Pépa in such a way that it would be for the last time we ever spoke, he responded, *"obviously not . . . or else you'd be here."*

I have a fear that these words will fail miserably in their attempt to calm a heart, however, to deny myself from writing them would be a disservice in displaying the care and compassion that is found towards you within my own.

Thus I shall trudge gingerly, but hard pressed enough in hopes that I leave a mark.

When our love is not reciprocated, when our love is scorned or deemed 'not enough' or simply rejected, something within our existence fractures. The most common of phrases is 'heart-broken', yet I've come to believe that the fracture exists within our mind and/or soul. We fail to grasp their reasoning (if any was given) and delve within our own worthiness and begin to question our very core with 'what's wrong with me?', 'am I not worth it?'.

The illness of a heart solicits depths of emotion beyond those occasioned by human infirmity - there's not a pill that calms or cures - there's not a 'aha' moment when it clicks and you're now over it - there's not a memory forgotten that doesn't leave a pit in the bottom of your stomach. The pain blackens your mind, sickens your dreams, and distorts the things once confirmed.

Dearest,
Having so many things that need and will be said, I pause to reflect on where to begin.
I've been sitting here with my dreadful pipe offering up smoke signals to the gods in hopes they may set me straight and yet their only consolation is this bravery to conclude my heart (us) in paper form.

After these following sentences, I shall promise you that all following letters will be in the utmost friendly vein. I want you to think not of me as a sore loser because I ploughed ahead and said the things that were nearest my heart even after you portrayed my role in your life to me. In time, I do hope you'll forgive me that much.

I am sorry that there was a certain abruptness about your departure - granted, it was not entirely without reason - yet nary a word you spoke of him or going. Last word I received from you would infringe on the definition of 'us' being together 'forever' - nevertheless, whether twas a lie or a miscalculation on my part, a courteous farewell would've been welcomed - such would have appeased my wonderings and wanderings for the past four years. But, maybe you didn't know you were going with him or say anything about going with him until you knew for certain that you were going and maybe that occurred the day you left and hence you failed to relay that message to I.

Asked to write a brief biography of myself once, I deemed myself as a 'decorator of words'.

To some God grants wisdom, to some knowledge, perseverance, strength. God grants, to others, tools of a trade, hands to fix the stars or a broken arm or a spewing toilet. Oh but to me, God poked my belly button and filled me with words.

You and I are guilty of the same offense.

I dread the doctor or not so much the doctor, but the going to the doctor. Thus, when an ailment arises, I Google that ailment . . . of which that Google-ing informs me that I should have deceased yesterday. Google doesn't ask questions. Google doesn't require a history of prior sickness or a genetics background. Google simply takes your ailment, applies that ailment to fifteen thousand other ailments and plausible side effects and diagnoses you with impending death.

Now, the discovery of the ill-defined ways of Google were learnt in a recent episode in my own life.

With a right handed swipe and a quick peek-a-boo to see what I left behind, lo and behold I did find - speckled stool! White polka-dotted poop!

To save myself the embarrassment of calling
a doctor and relaying such information to a
secretary was beyond what my cool, calm, and
collected self could muster.

Hence, I Googled - only to be informed that:

    a) I had a parasite in my body,
       eating away at my very essence
    or
    b) I had contracted the c word that rhymes
       with 'Prancer'.

Now, let me rewind.
If . . . and this is a George Washington Monument
type of huge 'if' . . . if Google would have
prefaced a diagnosis with a common "sensical"
question in the form of, 'did you by chance eat
white rice last night?' . . .

We are sitting on the bathroom floor of your one
room efficiency; our backs against the pretend
wall of porcelain, beside the litter box where
Kitty had poor aim, waiting on a plastic stick
strategically balanced on the edge of the sink
to reveal itself in the form of a mathematical
equation.

When Judas concludes his legacy,
May he reward Mr. Buchanan with a mention;
Who, without aide, placed a .45 to his temple
And locked himself into eternity.

—three months earlier, after 22 years as a church
deacon, 21 years directing the church choir, and
33 years of being a dad,
watched his own son die of colon cancer.

watched him want to die . . .

---

in the hue of the moon,
they fall on me.
dropped
by the stork
or
the angel of death
on their way back
to being a forgotten dream.
syllables.
individually wrapped
like lovers chocolate
or
left in a wasted heap
like a one night stand's under garments.
tis my honor
or
duty
to pair the socks together,
matched,
after signing the waiver wire
consenting to the risk of their poison
or
potion.

Which prayer does God answer?

I, praying to know the truth to set me free,
while she knows the truth and prays that the
truth may never be known.

'Forever found. In your eyes.'
She lied.
To you.
Forever has a thousand names.
As many as the stars.

She loves the night sky;
searching for the light,
the shooting across the blackness of it all
and vanishing just as swiftly,
because only stars and dreamers
come out at night.
She has a mural of the constellations
on her ceiling,
and when it rains,
she can recite them one by one.

Forever found. In your eyes.
Mine too.

Everything is different the second after this
one,
when the worst fear,
confirmed,
of every parent screams
from beneath the soul,
freeing itself from the sequestered chains of
eternity sentenced the very moment of your
conception.

Tis more beautiful,
my shadow
than my reflection.

Forgets to do his chores, finds corners in
crowded rooms, loves to read to the end of the
first chapter, practices his autograph while the
teacher teaches, knows all the answers to all
the questions he'll never answer aloud, and when
prompted in the home, sheepishly says, 'Yes,
sir', grasping not a word.

Yesterday, instructed to 'get ready' for school
-clothes had been lain out, shoes prematurely
tied - all one had to do was slip in. Half an
hour past, found standing stark naked in his
bedroom, staring into his reflection, flexing in
countless contortious ways.

And we ask, what's wrong with him?

Hesitant to diagnose, to label, to judge, I
listen to his parent's concerns as he illustrates
a typical day before me with the least amount of
use of words. I pen in the observation block on
my formal note-taking pad: *Obviously brilliant!*

The mother quizzes, *'Does he have ADD? ADHD? Is
he autistic? Aspergers? Just gifted? Unique?'*

And I responded, *'tis up to you if he's a weed or
a wildflower. A diamond or a piece of coal. But
to me, he seems more dreamy than distracted. More
blessed than burden.'*

'You never were as dashing as that night', she quipped.
'So you pray-tell that I peaked in August of '67, ay?'
'Afraid so!"

And that was the language of granny and pepa. Junior Pack died in March of 2000. Junior was driver-license-less his entire life. As my memory serves, Granny revved up that Cadillac with the extra-ruffled blue seat cushion in the passenger seat and drove Pepa to the ends of any world Pepa desired. I asked him once why he never acquired such - his response, *gives me a reason to sit beside of her anytime I want.'*

I am writing to you, my dear.

I am writing to you so you will know everything about me: who I am, who I've become. Would you even recognize me if I whispered your name in your ear?

Do you know what I've been through, what I've lost and found, since you kissed my lips with a tender lie for the last time?

That kiss is now me, a lie unto thyself.

I lie awake daydreaming of existing in your memories as you prance in mine?

I live in fear. Fear of leaving where you last knew I existed. I reason my procrastination with 'what if you come searching me?'

Some nights he needs directions and thus she
fiddles a map and instructs him which way to
turn, where to idle, where to speed and when to
brake.

Instinctual, yet the pathway thru those mountains
meanders - some nights on the back of a camel,
some on the concourse of a maiden voyage, and
others like a spell with a churn - slow, smooth,
and sweetly.

Some nights only just began, he pulls into
a vacant parking lot behind a twice removed
department store and loses his cool because he's
lost - he's always lost.

But surprisingly (however rarely), he finds an
undomesticated freeway and he let's go - he's
found the right key, sets the cruise to stroke
the perfect chord, and forgets he's at the wheel.

Tis on a night like this that no one attempts
to steer for fear of over-correcting. Thus, we
bumble thru the night, gripping and grimacing
this present darkness until . . .

Until the tumbleweeds and breath separate us.
Resting on its hood, we crawl thru imaginary
windows into a field of daisies where we cling to
one another before we depart.

Once she found a dry bone in this field.
Another, she found a diamond ring.

Your love story? Your love story begins with you - no one has ever loved you before more than when you first loved yourself.

In the past twelve hours, twelve trees have died at my fingertips. Litter lingers as notebook white snowflakes on my fake hardwood floors because that nor this sentence is as beautifully choreographed as McCarthy's road, as descriptive as Lewis's Narnia, as intertwined as eleven minutes with Coehlo, or as splendidly simple as Seuss's things. Even as I push buttons to create this sentence, as encouragement, I'm reminding myself that there are others who have not written such timelessness, that have sang the wrong note, stroked the wrong piano key, but then again, not all choruses can be as 'Amazing Grace' - evoking the oceans to tide, or the sinner to repent, or goose-bumps to skate figure eights down your vertebra.

I'm attracted to living or the idea of living. Being enveloped in life and life abundantly. Leaping without wings, finding deliriously happy, dancing like a dervish. When I was eight, I had a moment on the mountain beside my grand-parents house where I ran down that mountainside with all my might, so fast and free, that my jog became a tumble, and once my roll ceased and I found my footing, I laughed with the gods. I've been trying to recreate that feeling ever since.

That there might be words to describe un-mentionable feelings or a sentence for un-graspable emotions, or a paragraph for lost longings, is how writing can make one feel less alone in this world. In essence, you may not belong here or there, but you have paper and that paper rejects a nary thought of yours - a nary touch. Even when you've been a butthole your entire life, there is a one subject spiral notebook with perforated edges, sold at your local Walmart for 17 cents that will give you 70 chances to be loved by someone, unbeknownst to you, that does not give a rat's butt that you're a butthole.

The power of words, of writing, of books, allows one to venture into another you. Your imagination is uncaged, unjudged, uninhibited. You're free to roam about the country, with no expiration of miles or mind - you just go and let go.

The fog-filled bathroom made my visibility null. That's the thing with long, steamy showers - delightful, relaxing, yet lufa's can only scrub so much of yesterday away til the fog fills the air and murkies your view of what you're trying to remove. And it was my fault - I left the drawer open looking for a fresh Bic - but now my knee finds the corner of that drawer and I'm overwhelmed with a feeling of despair as I drop to the floor.

I want to scream 'daddy' to help rub out the pain but I know he can't hear me.

And in three days, I'll be screaming 'uncle' . . . can it really be 15 years?

I've lived on this floor for more minutes of my life than anywhere else and nicking my knee is the happiest of reasons why I'm down here. I have this loathsome belief that 'God hates me' which lingers as a cloud of locusts and I'm the crop

just waiting to be gulped. I feel like a wave
without an ocean, a star without a sky, an orphan
who knows too much.

I know where my dad is - I laid flowers beside
his rock yesterday - but the silence of this
hallway is all I have to remind me that he is
gone, and only silence hugs me when his memory
knocks on my door.

Why did I beg him for ice cream? Why did he walk?
Why did I watch? Why me? Why my dad?

Fifteen years of why's. If I could just walk down
my street, if I could just get past that street
light, I could conquer the world. But I can't
even get out of my bathroom without hurting.
And another day dies without my dad.

'Alice' witnessed her dad's murder from her
painted pink bedroom window. 'Alice' was 6 years
old. 'Alice' never made it past that streetlight.
'Alice' took her own life four months after this
diary entry. In honor of her, in honor of all
those who have a streetlight in their way, you're
not alone.

She who never holds my hand; she who was never
mine from the start. I don't even know what side
would please she and I fail giving up recognizing
she in the surging tide of the next moment.

. . . their flashing neon light read 'God is
love', thus my expectation rose from lost to
found, yet their place of worship was adorned
with poorly lit chandeliers and crooked crosses.
The accusation before the congregation was
pronounced in a hostile, insulting tone and I
soon learned this sacrilegious ceremony had
been a premeditated preparation to silence
me. The followers had no intention of loving
my difference; of living their definition.
Their minds were broken, stuck on repeat of
intolerance.

August reminds me you are gone. Breathing too.

. . . the bullet left a hole in his face
small enough to fit a matchbox car thru.
. . . it shattered silky skin, milk bone, and
pink drywall; busted Marc Jacobs frames into
needles and lifted mind over matter up onto the
ceiling fan.

. . . the pond of blood from the child's father
depicts a vulgar da Vinci: a mustache alone
near the doorway, an eye unclosed still staring,
while a medic named Derek bows his head to catch
his tears before touching pieces of a hope
untouched.

I know God must lurk in this crowd, as I do,
confused by the violent courage to simply cease;
when among the sirens and voices,
the bare-feet of a running wife and a bald boy
echo against eternity, blink, and find you gone.

Lord,
breathe in the noise
by which I bow to you;
and forgive me the gestures
grown within me
in your absence;
and grant me the courage
to become such a part of You that we forget me.

Lord,
lean on me,
even if I nourish myself with salt and sand;
and swing low and listen to my life
by which I borrow from you;
and grant me the patience
to bless those idols who are false with their
stained hands and those converts who are zealous
to confirm their contraire;
and let it be that my waiting be without
hesitation.

. . . she was my coloring book . . .
the beautiful mess in my mind.
. . . she was my coloring book . . .
the color outside the lines.

. . . she was my coloring book . . .
all ninety six colors in one number two.
. . . she was my coloring book . . .
every memory found in the late-night hue.

. . . I was her coloring book . . .
. . . painted black . . .
sealed blue.

On her way home, she usually bought a cup-o-joe
at the local cafe. It was her nightly treat.
Sometimes she asked for a splash of flavor,
sometimes not. The reasoning behind such requests
were webbed in a vast difference of emotions.
If flavor was added, she scurried home swiftly,
for company was on its way. If her cup was
flavorless, her stroll led to an inevitable
loneliness.

Today, she passed the cafe by. Unlocked a door to
an empty house and an unlit room - closetlike,
suffocating on stuff that fades, frays, and
forgets - and climbed the stairs to a half attic.
Tied a knot at the appropriate length and reached
inside her pocket, grabbing the box that forever
came out of. She unclasped the clasp without
looking, and laid the ring inside. Upon her
clasping back that forever box, she thought she
heard someone crying.

And then she leapt.

. . . asleep?
like coals - if perfectly blown into
could produce life.

. . . i touched her hand;
(you can predict a woman's age by her hands)
then i knew, she'd never hold mine again
. . . (you can't hold what isn't there).

. . . i knelt by the cold steel,
pressing my cheek to her cheek -
(she always wore Red Door - such a cheap perfume)
that smell is all i hope to remember.

. . . checked into the hotel
he saw her last.
next door
to the mountain
between
North and Tennessee

. . . swallowed
a refills worth
of Voltaren
seeking to forget.

. . . failed to kill him
- only left him
in a coma.

unable to speak,

still able
to
think.

Three stacked quarters. Turn clockwise. Mango
scented? Bargained for a bag, and got a boy.

Jack be careful. Jack be quick. Jack be worried,
she's about to pee on a stick.

I'd say my parents are proud of who I am and what
I've done, but wonderfully underwhelmed.

Oh Chimney Chimney let me rest
Lay me down and burn my chest
Tear my tears and breathe my best
Oh Chimney Chimney let me rest

Double knotted and naked by time and age
My heart you catch, your bye my cage
My mind props this prodigal's stage
All fields look the same

Oh Chimney Chimney let me rest
Lay me down and burn my chest
Tear my tears and breathe my best
Oh Chimney Chimney let me rest

One foot back and two eyes down
Life isn't lived when lived in bounds
The stars have fallen from your crown
All nights feel the same

Oh Chimney Chimney let me rest
Lay me down and burn my chest
Tear my tears and breathe my best
Oh Chimney Chimney let me rest

Dusted and busted, while I climb
Rigid and rusted, rotting my mind
Planted a tree on what was mine
All timbers sound the same

So Chimney Chimney let me rest

. . . So Chimney Chimney let me rest

_____

Tis devastating to want something more for someone than they want for themselves.

Few are the people we allow to be honest with us - that honesty that enacts change or action - that prompts us to gather our belongings and leave the comfortable for the unknown - that can not only read our disguises like child books, but flip the page to a better beginning.

I had shared the above scribble with my heart bare and vulnerable. He mumbled the word 'lost' repeatedly. Then quipped, *'all that which was lost is here in this room.'* I nodded, understanding his play on words, and responded with a grand line I penned long ago, *'but how do you put the puzzle of you together when you don't even recognize the pieces?'* He answered, *'You, first, have to be willing to pick up a piece.'*

She was frozen.
She wrestled with honesty because before my bluntness incurred, she had been shared fluffy fluff that fades with fleeting vapor. I had stripped away the fuzziness and what was left to greet her was the harsh reality behind the magnitude of such a decision. Concerning the subject of abortion, I returned her reply with the following - *which is scarier - hearing a child's voice yell out with adoration "mommy" or having your conscience brand you a "murderer"?*

Trace my tree down either branch to the roots of names I do not know and faces I do not recognize, and yet a thread of *Him* will be acknowledged from there to here. I am the here. From the time I was thirteen years old, it was clear to me that I would study theology. Being raised in a godly home, by godly parents; studying in a Christian school, listening in a Baptist church; my foundation of me was this *Him*, yet I'm not quite certain I even liked *Him*, or the *Him* I was force-fed thru a strangled straw.

The *Him* I was given suffocated you with rules and regulations, three point sermons and bulletin worship, cliques and social inequality, unexplained traditions and puppet programs, miraculous stories but poor examples. Mine eye hath seen the worst of Sunday saints and week-long whores. (Come to think of it, they were even whores on Sundays. Only difference was the difference between a Bible and ball in their hand!). I've witnessed the Bible being so twisted and deformed, piece-milled apart by vultures, that what remained was a stinking, rotting carcass of a cringing Christ. Bonhoffer's brother once said, the church is a *"poor feeble, boring, petty bourgeois institution."* I began to believe this in '97, for my first journal entry of that year read, "Christ is for Christians, not Christianity."

I'm not able to make it on my own . . . alone is
a frightful place; holding another's hand - not
as frightful!

. . . on our backs
with nothing but the blacktop to keep us warm;
upside down,
the dippers pour out stars like a tear-filled
storm.
She reaches
for my hand as Orion grasp his shield,
whispers, 'there are no stars in Raleigh,
just bright lights that fail to fill . . .'

. . . asked,
'so what do you aim for when there's no stars to
see?'
'I aimed for your hand; you must first believe.'

You will find me walking alone
down the street like a leashed dog -

caged, frozen, tied to a past,
on my knees begging to be let go,
whimpering questions to an unforgiving wind.

And if I do stop my stroll,
I can't help but dig in the highest of hopes
of burying you!

I change my mood for you
I shed my skin in seasons
I lack the grace you give
See here . . . here are the reasons

One: self-inflicted
Two: a bump in the night
Three: she let go
And I gave up the trappings of a fight

So I hang my heart to dry
And wave the merriest of goodbyes
I'm ready for you to see
This secret I hid inside

The man you thought I'd be
To the boy who never believed
From a could've been to a should've been
The hardest part lingers in the waiting on the
when

I've got my finger on this breaking dam
But I need you to hold up who I am
Because the dirt room where I hide
Has become the mess of a mud slide

Every thought you ever spent
Is being cashed in
The God of mine comes crashing in
I've gone farther than I ever wanted to go
But I'm coming home again

The seasons have fallen
The dam gives way
I changed my clothes for this
I hope you stay!

I love her . . .
. . . over there . . .   . . . much more,
. . . than here.

. . . I have unearthed - I do not love you . . .
. . . oh, how I wanted to - please, believe that
is true, but the idea of you trumps the skin of you.

. . . he hides from you
in an effort to keep his heart
from staining the carpet.

. . . he closes his eyes
with a deliberate determination
forgetting to forget,

. . . yet the veins behind
all lead like blue road maps
to an ocean of regret.

. . . this heart has been painted
blue red yellow black white
pick a flavor
layers of cake has gathered itself upon
and there is no sole solution
no clay key
no color compromise
that shall rinse the stain of you
from what is left

On the subject of love:
. . . her eyes eluded mine,
like waves that are always leaving -
and that's when I knew:
she was so ready to risk it all . . .
so ready to be hurt.

1402 Grandview Road:
I sat on the shore like a pupil,
gleaning the doctrine of the duck,
and found God's fingerprint,
wading in the muck.

As she washed herself,
I watchfully wondered -
when will you realize,
the night sticking to your insides,
can't be washed off? . . .

. . . only forgiven.

You reached into my chest,
pulled out a bleeding beating heart -
I've never fallen for anyone,
you've had me from the start.

A scattered dream, a great gatsby,
a charlotte's web harvested all my lost memories.

Find me at seven -
find me when you're thru.
I don't know where we're headed,
but I wanna go there with you!

Having sat thru a tutorial in the fine art of vague specifics, I left the classroom dejected.

I believe in specifics. Not an *alluding to* or a *draw your own conclusion*, or an *in time it shall be known* type of specifics, but bare-knuckle, this is my blood, this is how I feel about this or that specifics.

I trust them, like I trust myself to take this next breath. And this next one. And this one too! Breathing is a life being built - so are specifics . . . one thought, one word, one act at a time.

And beyond breathing, love is all about specifics. Love is about seeing, hearing, feeling, smelling, touching, and less about wondering and thinking. In perfect love, you do not have to wonder or talk of its existence, because it is. In perfect love, you can feel it in their touch, you can share it in the way they listen, you can witness it by the way they behold one another. Love is in the simplest of facts, of sentences - as in "I miss you", "I choose you", "you make me smile!" Love is a choice and in making that choice one has the opportunity to be generic, which in turn will cost a beloved's faith, or one may choose specifics, which will garner our beloved's trust. Specifics lead to freedom, whereas the lack of specifics complicates and holds captive your own heart.

The white lie of christianity

I was sold a product that was free . . .
Standing under the street-lamp, reverberating in
the alley, *"Free gift. Free gift. Free gift. No*
purchase necessary. Limit one per customer. Free
gift. Free gift. Free gift".

Free. Free. Free. Whether Webster knew the chaos
he would create when creating this four-letter
word, our society sprints to whomever or whatever
screams "free". Inevitably, we may not partake
of the "free" substance, but we'll peek at it -
inquire, ask a few questions, get to know "free"
item a little better, maybe even hold its hand.

I accepted "free gift" with a shallow hesitance
and now, odd years removed from that acceptance,
I am bound by the chains of that "free gift".

My art work drips of years of replicated fears
Where everything is brilliant from the ground
You tipped me over sunlight's edge
Now gravity pulls me down
down
down
I once was a fire
I turned into ice

The ending of the scar crawled its way to the
inside of his elbow - my beady eyes dove thru
his skin and my mouth asked, *"how do you keep a*
secret when it is written all over the blackboard
of your soul?"

I have sat in circles with legends of the
Faith. I have stood in the footprints on their
platforms, waving my banner of agreement. I
have pursued their education with zeal. I have
memorized their declarations, mimicked their
antics, and missed their mark!

I have failed to grasp the realization behind the
box the church and its appointees have placed
itself into. Thus, being on the outside, peering
through tarnished glass, I have been branded a
backwards Christian – even a hypocrite.

This branding was self-inflicted with pride. I
am not ashamed to bear my scar, yet my platform
for a show-n-tell display is null. Nonetheless,
as an outlet to scream, I grip my pen to write my
showing from the beginning.

The iron was heated when I began to doubt and
question all that I was "misled" to believe. I
am an eye-witness to the arguments, the debates,
the accusations, the slandering's between
theologians and atheists, between denominations
and religions, between the pulpit and the pew,
between the pew and the person sitting next to
me! Killing us softly from His existence to
His non-existence, from Creation to evolution,
from His virgin birth to illegitimacy, from
His resurrection to His shroud, from His
words written in red to musings of mad men,
from pastor's rights to the abuse of those
rights, from public theatres to Blockbuster,
from attendance in buildings to a personal
relationship, from culottes to dukes, from Heaven
to Hades to Hell, from the seven deadly sins to
equality, from gluttony to fasting, from public
prayer to prayer closets, from husbands and wives

to submission and slavery, from child respect to regardless obedience, from the suffering of the good to the blessing of the bad.

More could be painted yet for the sake of brevity, my portrait begins to dry, but my conclusion to the matter is written in sand for the waves of any and every ocean to wipe away. From Biblical doctrine to personal conviction to my pen, the arguments within Christianity stopped being about God long ago. Christianity isn't four walls, or boxes, or opinions - it is God and the belief that He is God. He didn't quip I am here or I am there - He is limit-less, box-less, wall-less, and He doesn't care what your opinion is - so to quote His sovereignty, He is "I am"! So take your box and . . . please, please, please recycle.

Betrayal is witnessing the love of your life, marrying the love of her life.

The worse part about going thru a shoebox is remembering being proud of crap like this. Even worse is not being able to pretend that I wasn't proud of it.

I've learned that we cling to our fairy fables until the price for believing in them becomes too high.

I've learned that you can pass the bread basket and clench secrets you'll never share, in the same hand.

. . . my words, written last evening, were from a heart laid bare for all to plunder. I write to release my own sanity, realizing that I have much to learn, to gain, to understand, thru others that respond and reflect their own understandings. Noting that acknowledgment and the "outcome" of the messages therein, a "friendly, circular" debate could be had, with nothing more than words wasted and disagreement gained! Much of my "note" was derived from a Biblical foundation, alike many of the comments that have been posted. Nothing so irritates me more than an ignorant Christian that hides behind an "out-of-context" Bible. Furthermore, the Bible is not a blueprint upon which Christians can wave their authority as dictators above the law or as knowing the will of God. Diving into the shallowest waters of the Bible, it is evident that war is not a 21st century invention. War and the testimonies of dead men litter the pages of the Testaments, and even so, God orchestrated the deaths of some of those men.

I am an advocate of free-will, and that free-will has led us to our location, today. I have chosen my path. Alike, he has chosen his. You have chosen yours. But that same common thread runs between us all, being "created in His image", and being of "one blood". What began in the Garden, toppled at the Tower of Babel, and rained down on the third floor of a hut in Pakistan is the culmination of our exploitation of that freewill - nothing more, nothing less!

he hangs as mistletoe:
for all who see -
peck death.
my reflection hid in his stare
looking out from the inside
of the bottom of a well,
empty.

his pupils -
frozen black dots.
dilated pearls.
a black hole
resembling a mouth,
open,

locked
in a scream.
drowning in a sky
so black,
alone.

lost
in the space
between
you and i.

darkness falls asleep in the eye
and never wakes
until

darkness
meets

the dawn.

Sometimes death is not as tragic as not knowing how to live.

I've done a lot nothing, pretending to be doing something.

I've wasted much time telling others things I've since forgotten. Furthermore, I've promised things I've known I couldn't keep.

I've had conversations that un-wrapped the reality that we aren't friends anymore, and thus, I ended the conversation with a period, instead of a comma.

I've cut myself to bleed out my pain. I only lost a portion of myself in the process.

I've uncovered that I'm meaner to myself than another has ever dared.

I've prayed prayers tempting God to answer and prove Himself. When He answered "wrongly", I questioned if I ever believed.

I've written my obituary seven times. Six ended as trash. My first draft remains.

I like to remember things the way I remember them, not necessarily the way they happened.

I stared into a mirror and came to terms with the undeniable fact that this is the face I will have the rest of my life.

I watched my granny die. It took 18 days. I wanted her to die. Until she did.

I ride a bike instead of doing drugs. My bike has oft kept me from accepting responsibility for myself.

I look people in the eye to catch a glimpse of their soul. I've peered into many soulless dots.

I asked myself, *"is feeling pain better than being numb?"*, *"is being dead better than running from demons past?"* I have no intentions of asking myself again. The answer scared me.

I must admit that it was great fun being cute. But one day, it just ended.

I believe the most sacred of places to touch is one's eyelids.

I've been quite busy forgetting to remember, but while I'm remembering, I'm praying to forget.

I received a card with a beautiful poem that read, "time heals all wounds". Time doesn't heal a memory.

I threw a rock at the sky once and yelled at God for not behaving the way I wanted Him too. He threw the rock back at me.

I look in vain within me for the writer who I compare myself with.

I have learned there are more ways to kill yourself than just with a gun, a rope, a knife or pills.

I laughed every time I kissed her because I was thinking to myself, *"your lips would make a lollipop very happy."* It takes 1317 some odd licks before you end up with only a stick.

I began to notice that like milk, everything has an expiration date. Inconveniently, not everything is stamped.

I am attempting to straighten all that I have made crooked.

I am better at holding someone's hand than I am at holding their heart.

You can't see stars, or reach for stars, when you're always looking down.

I leave my house for work at three fifteen am eastern. By the time the sun wakes up, I have tossed too many fifty pound bags of dog food into neatly stacked stacks for people to tip over so I can re-stack them and have a job. Before this endeavor, it had been years since I had lifted anything heavier than guilt.

I've learned that most people don't go to therapy. They simply go to work. I ride a bicycle.

I've learned that I have doubts about my doubts.

I've learned that I've had affairs with the grandest of hopes and dreams, only to awake to the marriage I've created.

. . . she pulled me out of me like roots out of
the ground.

. . . twas rather beautiful to behold – the
way he swam into her eyes and rescued all of
her dreams . . . the way he stayed through her
screams and starved all her insecurities . . .
the way he took her hand and sailed into forever.

. . . the fiction and the friction – it's the sum
of what we've become.
. . . when we bought a lie and changed for no
reason, other than it's easier to blink than to
disappear.

. . . I'd be dancing if I wasn't so desperate,
a little more understanding if I had the mind.
I could give you answers if I'd ask the questions
and if I thought I could, I'd turn back time.

. . . I guess if you look away, you can sleep;
but even from my knees, I caught you peek.
. . . this puddle of tears I've bled has become
an ocean you cannot cross.

. . . in response to a recent critic, I asked:
*"does it confuse you that I speak of death from a
personal relationship, and for sake of circles,
haunt you with these suicidal words, thinking, by
divine chance, that they will rub off on you and
possess a mere meaning for you (to you) as well?"*

---

conclusion

Today marks three years since I left that suicide note on my blue-enamel kitchen counter. I was unsure if I was going to make it home from my daily-self-medication-therapy of pedaling a bicycle.

(break)

I picked up a bicycle in May of 2010. Last night, I pedaled past mile marker twenty six thousand, six hundred and fifty. In May of 2010, I weighed two hundred and ten pounds. At the time of my slip and in the months shortly thereafter, I lost a third of who I was - seventy pounds. Standing centimeters shy from being seventy seven inches tall, I resembled a skeletal Casper.

(break)

I'd be lying if I told you I could remember much of those three years. I remember riding a bicycle. I remember writing everything you've already read. I remember crawling up my stairs into my bedroom and lying under my bed, attempting to hide my existence. I remember ruining my name, my relationships. I remember building walls no one could climb and moats no one could cross. I remember tucking myself into the miserable shell of the man I was and praying that the sun would boil me into eternity.

(break)

And hence, the snail.

June 19th of 2011, I walked the final quarter of
a mile home after pedaling some eighty plus miles
- my legs had quit and as I reached the edge of
my townhomes yard, I laid my bike in the ditch
and crawled towards my back door. Upon reaching
my back deck, a shell of a deceased snail tripped
my vision. Burnt, cracked, hollow - reminded me
of me.

(break)

Sprinkled with honor - our successes that
remind ourselves that we made a difference; our
accomplishments that we tout with pride; our
traits that we find desirable within ourselves;
our things that we hold near and dear to our
hearts that give us a reason to believe in
ourselves.

Speckled with horror - our failures that drench
our minds with doubt; our addictions that create
shame and embarrassment if anyone would see; our
frailty that hinders ourselves from letting go;
our mistakes that bind our futures in our pasts.

Spackled with hope - the difference in between
that honor and the horror within each of us;
the banner that gives us a second chance, a
third chance, a millionth chance; the courage to
live today for tomorrow; the light that beams
through the darkest night into a most glorious of
beginnings.

(break)

I have yet to complete treatment or even begin. I
am as sober as the day I was born. This mind of
mine will linger in my bones til forever comes,

but I've completed this book and just maybe, this
was step one in this thing called healing.
(break)

I have tried to tear myself open and expose all
that I ever tried to hide. I needed to break my
own silence and tell you who I was, what I've
done, where I've been.

(break)

I am Stephen Wolfe, Jr. I am defective. I
once slipped. I once was lost. But now I am
found. Jesus loves me this I know. He loves you
too . . .
as do I.

(break)

Forward this snail marches on.